On the Sonnets of Robert Frost

On the Sonnets of Robert Frost

A Critical Examination of the 37 Poems

by
H. A. MAXSON

McFarland & Company, Inc., Publishers
Jefferson, North Carolina, and London

The present work is a reprint of the library bound edition of On the Sonnets of Robert Frost: A Critical Examination of the 37 Poems, *first published in 1997 by McFarland.*

LIBRARY OF CONGRESS CATALOGUING-IN-PUBLICATION DATA

Maxson, H.A.
   On the sonnets of Robert Frost : a critical examination of the 37 poems / by H.A. Maxson.
      p.   cm.
   Includes bibliographical references and index.

   ISBN 0-7864-2420-6 (softcover : 55# alkaline paper)

   1. Frost, Robert, 1874–1963 — Criticism and interpretation.
2. Sonnets, American — History and criticism.
PS3511.R94 Z7857   2005
811'.52 — dc21   97034951

British Library cataloguing data are available

©1997 H. A. Maxson. All rights reserved

No part of this book may be reproduced or transmitted in any form or by any means, electronic or mechanical, including photocopying or recording, or by any information storage and retrieval system, without permission in writing from the publisher.

On the cover: Robert Frost artwork *(USPS)*; background image ©2005 PhotoSpin.

Manufactured in the United States of America

McFarland & Company, Inc., Publishers
   Box 611, Jefferson, North Carolina 28640
   www.mcfarlandpub.com

For Maureen
For Carrie
For my parents
And for Thomas Reiter, whose eyes and ears
helped immeasurably to shape this book

Contents

Introduction	1
"The Strictest Form I Have Behaved In":	
Identifying Frost's Sonnets	
1 "An arrest of disorder": Frost's Forms and Themes	13
2 Into My Own: The Sonnets of *A Boy's Will*	21
Into My Own	23
A Dream Pang	28
The Vantage Point	31
3 Range-Finding: The Sonnets of *Mountain Interval*	35
Meeting and Passing	37
The Oven Bird	40
Putting in the Seed	44
Range-Finding	48
4 On a Tree...: The Sonnet of *New Hampshire*	51
On a Tree Fallen Across the Road	53
5 Acquainted with the Night: The Sonnets of	
West-Running Brook	59
Acceptance	61
Once by the Pacific	65
The Flood	69
Acquainted with the Night	72
A Soldier	77
The Investment	79

6	The Master Speed: The Sonnets of *A Further Range*	85
	The Master Speed	87
	Design	89
	On a Bird Singing in Its Sleep	94
	Unharvested	98
7	The Silken Tent: The Sonnets of *A Witness Tree*	101
	The Silken Tent	103
	Never Again Would Birds' Song Be the Same	106
	Time Out	109
8	Etherealizing: The Sonnets of *Steeple Bush*	113
	Etherealizing	115
	Why Wait for Science	116
	Any Size We Please	118
	The Planners	120
	No Holy Wars for Them	121
	Bursting Rapture	122
	The Broken Drought	123
9	Despair: Other Sonnets	127
	Despair	129
	When the Speed Comes	131
	The Mill City	133
	Pursuit of the Word	134
	The Rain Bath	135
	On Talk of Peace at This Time	136
	The Pans	138
	Trouble Rhyming	140
	A Bed in the Barn	141

Bibliography   145
Index   147

Introduction

"The strictest form I have behaved in"

Identifying Frost's Sonnets

Introduction: Identifying Frost's Sonnets

Critics have not yet dealt seriously with Robert Frost as a sonneteer. They have evaluated, analyzed and commented on individual sonnets, and at least one article, by Janis Stout, attempts to establish which poems are sonnets, but the sonnets as a separate corpus have not been thoroughly and uniformly examined solely in that context. We need to rectify this oversight because Frost's best sonnets are among the finest written in this century, or any century for that matter. These poems deserve the same serious treatment and high respect afforded the lyrics and dramatic dialogues and monologues.

The sonnet was the only fixed form Frost ever employed. That fact in itself should speak volumes about their importance and uniqueness in his body of work. (I am ignoring couplets, blank verse, terza rima and ballad stanzas because they are line or stanza forms, not whole-poem forms.) A sonnet variant was the first poem in his first book, and the direction of a good deal of his career was mapped out in *A Boy's Will*. Sonnet variants like "Into My Own" are the norm in Frost, and he announces this from page one. But more compelling is this: Fully eight sonnets are among the very best poems in *Complete Poems*.

The sonnets, like the rest of the poems, fall very nearly into the divisions Randall Jarrell devised in "To the Laodiceans": "[H]is *Complete Poems* have the air of being able to educate any faithful reader into tearing out a third of the pages, reading a third, and practically wearing out the rest" (41). But before we deal with the sonnets, let's first determine which of the poems are sonnets. This seemingly simple task becomes quite complicated in light of Frost's experimentation.

In Sara de Ford and Clarinda Harris Lott's *Forms of Verse*, the authors claim that: Robert Frost "wrote about twenty-seven [sonnets] including all the variants" (198). About twenty-seven? For over twenty years that statement has intrigued me. Did he write twenty-seven sonnets, or didn't he? You can estimate apples in a basket or attendees at a concert, but why would you estimate the number of sonnets in a collection? They're the ones with fourteen lines in iambic pentameter, aren't they? De Ford and Lott reprint a few of Frost's sonnets in their text and discuss a few others, but nowhere do they give a list of the "about twenty-seven." We are left with only the *Complete*

Poems, a calculator and precious little comment by Frost on what qualifies as a sonnet in his world.

What comment there is, however — in essays, letters and talks — is absolutely necessary to compile the list of sonnets. None of the major critics even suggest that the sonnets deserve separate recognition. Elaine Barry devotes a chapter to Frost's sonnets in her book *Robert Frost*, but she offers no list, and her discussions are limited to only a few poems. Janis Stout published "Convention and Variation in Frost's Sonnets," but she too stopped short of offering a definitive list. In a footnote she lists the number of sonnets she finds in each book, but she does not name all of them in her text.

So, how many sonnets are there? By my reckoning there are thirty-seven. Although I suspect some readers will dispute my choices and make strong claims for others, this list rejects any poems not fourteen lines long (and a few that are) and any that seem too far, metrically, from the norm Frost establishes in the poems that are inarguably sonnets despite their variant rhyme schemes or meters. There are not many strict sonnets in the traditional sense, but there are a few, and these seem to establish one boundary. The other boundary stands where the sonnets push the form to its limits and sometimes appear so much like the "failed" sonnets — often called "sonnet-like" — that it is difficult to tell one from the other. But here is where Frost's poetic theory, practice and statements about the form must be considered. Although his prose comments are few, and downright scarce on the sonnet itself, he has supplied enough that some fairly clear guidelines can be established.

In "The Figure a Poem Makes" Frost writes: "Like a piece of ice on a hot stove the poem must ride on its own melting." This is a statement of organic composition worthy of Coleridge. Applied to the sonnets, it suggests that we must not tie Frost down to conventional rhyme schemes.

Organic composition argues that a poem that "begins in delight and ends in wisdom" cannot simply stop in midmelt just because the word does not satisfy some established rhyme scheme. The sonnet may be the strictest form in use in English, but it is also the most flexible, which explains why it has survived nearly intact for seven hundred years or more, and continues as the most popular fixed form even in seemingly formless times.

Introduction : Identifying Frost's Sonnets

So, why is there no Frostian sonnet? Again, organic composition precludes such a thing. In the poems in general, and in the sonnets specifically, Frost rarely repeats rhyme schemes or metrical patterns, that is, quirky, personal patterns outside of "loose iambic or strict iambic." And the poems do not suffer for this constant reinvention. The uniqueness of each is one reason they fit most definitions of a modernist poem, despite their "sonnetness." Consequently, aberrant rhyme schemes are not a criterion for selecting the sonnets.

But pattern is. Some sonnet-like poems are not sonnets by dint of their lack of a discernible pattern. One of the elements that attracts poets to the sonnet is its overall design. Frost was an experimenter, but he was not an anarchist. Take away the design inherent in the sonnet, and you take away the sonnet. Reinvent the rhyme scheme, yes, but there must be form within the form — or else, I think Frost would say, you might as well write free verse. Furthermore, we must consider this from "The Figure a Poem Makes": The poem is "a momentary stay against confusion." A sonnet is inherently orderly. It creates form inside of chaos, and the lack of a rhyme pattern simply does not contribute to the orderliness. Although Frost never spoke directly to this matter, he seems, at least, to have addressed it indirectly in "The Constant Symbol," from which I quote below.

In all of the sonnets that are clearly sonnets there is a "turn." It is not always located in line nine or in line thirteen as the Italian and the English forms call for, but it is there. Like the rhyme scheme, the turn appears where it is called for organically. There is never a sense of manipulation to make the parts fit "as they are supposed to." But there is a sense that the elements of the sonnet appear as the logic of each poem develops. The "delight," to borrow Frost's term, in the sonnets is in *not* finding the turn where you expect it, but where you didn't expect it and thus discovering the rightness of its placement.

Length is the last criterion I applied to the selection of the sonnets. Some critics have attempted to make cases for various poems (discussed below), but none have made compelling arguments for their being anything more than sonnet-like. Frost was attracted to the shape of the sonnet. He called it a "cube," for its length and its width — it appears stocky and solid on the page — and for its challenge, its orderliness and, I suspect, a reason I have not seen proffered before: More than any other form, the sonnet looks like a window or a picture lying on the page. The form provided him the frame in which to create the pictures and the dramas the sonnets articulate. If we think about how often windows and other frames appear throughout the canon, and not just as barriers, it becomes apparent that the sonnet was another opportunity to exploit a naturalized form.

Some poems that others have labeled as sonnets do not appear on my list. At least one poem on my list may not appear on anyone else's. But I will deal with these in turn.

In 1961 Frost wrote to Louis Untermeyer: "The sonnet is the strictest form I have behaved in, and that mainly by pretending it wasn't a sonnet." And it is that "pretending" that complicates matters. One must determine how far was too far for Frost. How far would he go before crossing a kind of line between what was a sonnet and what was a sonnet-like poem? Yet despite the experimentation, the endless fiddling, Frost ultimately was fairly rigid in how he dealt with the form.

In "The Constant Symbol" he wrote:

> Suppose [Shakespeare] to have written down "When in disgrace with Fortune and men's eyes." He has uttered about as much as he has to live up to in the theme as in the form.... He may proceed as in blank verse. Two lines more, however, and he has set himself in for rhyme, three more and he has set himself a stanza.... His worldly commitments are now three or four deep. Between us, he was no doubt bent on the sonnet in the first place from habit, and what's the use pretending he was a freer agent than he had any ambition to be? He had made most of his commitments all in one plunge.... And worry is as to whether he will outlast or last out the fourteen lines — have to cramp or stretch to come out even — have enough bread for the butter or butter for the bread. As a matter of fact, he gets through the twelve lines and doesn't quite know what to do with the last two.
>
> Things like that and worse are the reason the sonnet is so suspect a form and has driven so many to free verse and even to the novel. Many a quatrain is salvaged from a sonnet that went agley.

From these comments it seems unlikely that Frost would consider a twelve- or thirteen-, a fifteen- or sixteen-line poem a sonnet. On the other hand, it seems quite possible that a good many sonnet-like poems were, at first drip, intended to be sonnets but somewhere went amiss. For example, "Hyla Brook" is immediately disqualified because it is fifteen lines long. Its rhyme scheme starts out promisingly, but after the opening *abba*, it tumbles into an organic collection of couplets and other patterns. The turn, if that is what it is, at line twelve is vague. The truest turn occurs in line fifteen — but that, alas, comes across as a mere tag line, one that could have appeared at the end of any number of poems. "The Gift Outright," also occasionally called a sonnet, cannot be a sonnet, according to the criteria established obliquely from Frost, because it is sixteen lines long. And what's more, it is blank verse.

I have no doubt that both of these poems owe a heavy debt to the sonnet, and to Frost's credit he did not sacrifice what they wanted to be for what he wanted them to be. He left them alone, nodded to Petrarch and Shakespeare, and moved on, a sonnet less in the load, but still true to his organic theories.

On the other hand, there are two fourteen-line poems often considered sonnets; indeed, in the *Voices and Visions* series, for example, the narrator calls "Mowing" a sonnet, as do many critics, including Pritchard, Barry, Stout and others. But read carefully it simply does not *act* like a sonnet, or at least not like any other Frost sonnet. By this I mean that it does not develop an idea, expand on it, twist it around, give an anecdote then comment on it, sum up or pronounce philosophically in an epigrammatic couplet, or do any of the things we expect of a sonnet — by Frost or any other poet. It does not turn, either at line nine or thirteen; in fact, it does not turn, clearly and decisively, at all. Frost was not a slave to the position of the turn (as has already been established), but all of his obvious sonnets, and even his cagey variants, do turn — somewhere. And that is a significant point. It is a convention or tradition that Frost would not ignore. Apparently it is one point that can be counted on in any poem "pretending" to be a sonnet. The rhymes in "Mowing" are arbitrary (*abcabdecdfegfg*) and thoroughly unlike any other "sonnet" Frost wrote. It could be argued that "Acquainted with the Night," which employs terza rima for its stanzas, is also unlike any other Frost sonnet, but there, at least, there is a pattern. Rhyme in "Mowing" is not patterned at all.

If there is any remaining doubt, look at "The Vantage Point" in *The Complete Poems*. That poem, unquestionably a sonnet, typifies the kind of care Frost took even with his most experimental sonnets. Paul Fussell singles it out and spends two pages discussing just the masterfulness of the turn in his excellent *Poetic Meter and Poetic Form*.

"Mowing" is the single most troublesome of the sonnet-like poems because it is aberrant, and because so many critics have called it a sonnet without discussing what makes it so. Those who have looked closely seem only partly convinced. Elaine Barry calls "Mowing" a sonnet but does not discuss it. Janis P. Stout lists "Mowing" as a sonnet and discusses it briefly, but begins by calling it "the most irregular of the sonnets." She claims there are two

> minor turns ... after the sixth and eighth lines, so that the seventh and eighth ... constitute a fulcrum on which the poem balances, a transition from the opening six lines, musing on what the scythe might be whispering, to the closing six, suggesting that the pleasure of purposeful action is its own meaning [35].

Syntactically these lines belong to lines nine through fourteen, yet their rhymes connect line seven with line eleven, and eight with three. But rather than a fulcrum, they look more like a wedge driven between the physical first six lines and the philosophical last six. I do not see this as a turn in any conventional sense. A transitional space, yes, but not a turn. The second half of the poem employs different language and sounds different from the first six lines, but again, look at "The Vantage Point" and you will see the obvious difference. I think we have an early attempt at a sonnet that failed.

I would certainly place "Mowing" among the one-third of Frost's poems that should be worn out, but it does not appear on my list of sonnets.

A later poem, which most certainly should be on anyone's cast-off list, is also fourteen lines but, again, is not a sonnet. "To the Right Person" appears in the "Editorials" section of *Steeple Bush,* the book that contains the highest concentration of sonnets anywhere in Frost's canon. No elaborate argument, no in-depth look at the prosody of this poem is needed. We need only look at the seven poems in the "Editorials" that are clearly sonnets to see that this poem only coincidentally achieved meltdown at line fourteen.

"Unharvested," from *A Further Range,* is a poem I suspect few readers, offhand, would consider a sonnet, if they knew it at all. At first glance the poem appears to have a very irregular rhyme scheme, but a closer look reveals that it is less irregular and intricate (*abacbc-dade edff*). What is irregular is the meter. The poem can be scanned as tetrameter using nineteen anapests and two dactyls in the process. However, that meter is highly unusual for Frost, there being no precedent I can recall. Scanning it another way reveals an irregular but much more Frostian iambic pentameter line with abundant variation, use of catalexis and two lines of blatant tetrameter. With either scansion I would hold out for its sonnet qualities. And nowhere does Frost comment on line length in the sonnet, only on poem length. Unlike the poems previously discussed, this one does act like a sonnet. It falls into Jarrell's middle group. It does not need to be worn out, but it doesn't deserve to be torn out either.

But how can I justify the poem as a sonnet if it can be scanned as tetrameter or as irregular pentameter? The answer is by precedent, by the clear turn, by closure, and by association.

As far as precedent, I'm sure there are many other examples, but let me just mention a few. Shakespeare's "Sonnet 145" is tetrameter — "Those lips that love's own hand did make." And Elinor Wylie, a contemporary with whom Frost was familiar, wrote what she called "little sonnets," that is, sonnets written in iambic tetrameter. Couple that with this statement from a letter Frost wrote to Lewis B. Chase in 1917: "But before all write me as one who cares most for Shakespearean and Wordsworthian sonnets." Altogether, I think there is justification for labeling "Unharvested" a sonnet. If it is jagged pentameter, the turn, at line eleven, is at once obvious — the tone and diction become prayerful — and subtle. Having just compared fallen, unharvested apples to the fall of man, Frost gives the line the only feminine ending in the poem. So that there is no mistake about his intentions, he carries the rhyme over from the previous stanza, not once, but twice.

Closure also makes this poem a sonnet for me — not just sonnet-like, but the genuine article. The closing quatrain is epigrammatic, strongly iambic pentameter, and deftly returns us to the olfactory image of the opening.

Lastly, there is the argument by association. I suggest that "Unharvested" is a companion piece to "The Oven Bird." I am convinced that the poem tests the limits of the form (perhaps more than any other) and tells us straight out that it will do so: "And come to leave the routine road...."

"The Oven Bird" invites us in with its song. "Unharvested"

invites us in with scent. Both offer showers of vegetation heaped on the ground—leaves and blooms in one, leaves and fruit in the other. Both build to a reference to the biblical Fall just prior to the turn, and both address diminished things. Whereas "The Oven Bird" ends on that note, "...what to make of a diminished thing," "Unharvested" attempts an answer.

What to make of a diminished thing? A mystery, a moment unplanned, unscheduled. A surprise within the everyday, something "we forgot we knew."

Fortunately the remaining sonnets present few of the problems addressed so far. Many appear over and over in articles and books paired up with the term "sonnet," and I have no argument with any of them, regardless of the use of couplets, triplets, or terza rima. The blending of forms, like the blending of styles, voices, metrics and so forth, is today a commonplace. Although not solely responsible for this development, Frost was certainly influential and gave the practice credence. For Frost there was still plenty of room for experimentation within the confines of traditional rhyme and meter.

Judging by the many poems in the 1984 anthology *Strong Measures* that "pretend" to be various fixed forms, Frost's practices have been taken to heart by later generations of poets. Of the nine methods of experimentation the editors of *Strong Measures* identify, at least four of them can be traced back to Frost: "disguising forms," "shifting stanzaic patterns," "creating hybrid forms," and "inventing nonce forms." Although Frost almost certainly borrows the impulse from many sources, his use of these practices validated them for a great many poets who followed.

It isn't that the sonnet would not have survived into the twentieth century without Frost. It certainly would have. The fact that the sonnet has outlasted revolutions and periods of disuse and disregard proves that the form is not only flexible, adaptable and portable (from language to language); it is also a survivor. When poets Octavio Paz, Jacques Roubaud, Eduardo Sanguineti and Charles Tomlinson gathered in Paris in April 1969 to write their *Renga*, it was the sonnet they chose to use—not the venerable haiku, but a Western form, one pliable enough to be shaped (and reshaped) by many hands simultaneously. I have never for a moment wondered why Frost was attracted—why anyone is attracted—to the sonnet. It is the embodiment, both in shape and lyrical demands, of the personal lyric that has been the hallmark of English-speaking poetry since the Romantics salvaged it from its low regard at the end of the neo-classical age. In the words of Octavio Paz, "it is the sole traditional form which has remained alive up to our own times" (*Renga* 25).

Elaine Barry suggests that Frost was attracted to the sonnet because it offered form in a world otherwise dominated by chaos and insanity — in his sister, Jeanie, his daughter, Irma, his son, Carol, and occasionally perhaps in himself.

Whatever the attraction was, he returned to the form twenty-eight times in the 345 poems he chose to collect in *The Poetry of Robert Frost*— the volume contains *In the Clearing*, *The Complete Poems* does not — which is 8 percent of the total. Not counting the *Masque* books, sonnets appear in seven of nine books — none in *North of Boston* or *In the Clearing*. An additional nine sonnets were posthumously published in *Frost: Collected Poems, Prose and Plays*. These will be discussed in Chapter 10.

Here then is my list of the sonnets of Robert Frost by volume.

A Boy's Will 1913
  "Into My Own," "A Dream Pang," "The Vantage Point"
Mountain Interval 1916
  "Meeting and Passing," "The Oven Bird," "Putting in the Seed," "Range-Finding"
New Hampshire 1924
  "On a Tree Fallen Across the Road"
West-Running Brook 1928
  "Acceptance," "Once by the Pacific," "The Flood," "Acquainted with the Night," "The Soldier," "The Investment"
A Further Range 1936
  "The Master Speed," "Design," "On a Bird Singing in Its Sleep," "Unharvested"
A Witness Tree 1942
  "The Silken Tent," "Never Again Would Birds' Song Be the Same," "Time Out"
Steeple Bush 1947
  "Etherealizing," "Why Wait for Science," "Any Size We

Please," "The Planners," "No Holy War for Them," "Bursting Rapture," "The Broken Drought"
Frost: Collected Poems, Prose and Plays 1995
"Despair," "When the Speed Comes," "The Mill City," "Pursuit of the Word," "The Rain Bath," "On Talk of Peace at This Time," "The Pans," "Trouble Rhyming," "A Bed in the Barn."

I mentioned earlier my belief that eight of the sonnets are candidates for immortality. Making such nominations is of course a crapshoot, but judging by the reputation these poems have gained and kept since they first appeared, I would bet that posterity will continue to treat them well — not because they are sonnets, not even because they are Robert Frost's, but because they are among the best and most important poems written this century: "Design," "The Silken Tent," "Acquainted with the Night," "Once by the Pacific," "The Oven Bird," "Putting in the Seed," "Into My Own," and "Never Again Would Birds' Song Be the Same."

A few years could see a dramatic shift in what we now consider the essential Frost. But regardless of which poems survive, it seems apparent that at least a few of the sonnets will be among them.

The sonnets are an important part of the Frost canon. They stand out just as distinctly as the monologues and dialogues and the lyrics. They stand out not just when they are "pretending" to be sonnets but also when they are playing by the rules. They appear in significant places in the canon — as the first poem in *A Boy's Will* and as a forum for social comment in *Steeple Bush*. When he sought to show his affections for Elinor, his daughter, and Kay Morrison, he chose the sonnet.

At any rate, any list established now is at best speculation due to the nature of his theories and practices of composition. The best we have to go on are Frost's comments in letters and talks and assumptions based on theoretical remarks, scant as they may be. Ultimately the poems stand or fall on their own merits regardless of what form or tradition they fall into, neatly or otherwise. What is important is that we have the poems — the good, the bad, and the agley — and no amount of speculation or assuming can change that.

Chapter 1

"An arrest of disorder"

Frost's Forms and Themes

Perhaps the most famous of Robert Frost's definitions of a poem is "a momentary stay against confusion." I would like to discuss three points in regard to this statement and the sonnets. One, that by choosing and remaining true to poetic practices that were under attack during his career, Frost extended his "momentary" to a lifetime, rejecting the "confusion" of his contemporaries, namely the free-verse poets, who were recreating form for every new poem. Two, that "momentary," for Frost, was a matter of space, not time. Each poem became a "stay" to be returned to again and again, not merely a lucid moment in time to be left behind. And three, Frost's "confusion" became, in Randall Jarrell's terms, on of his "obsessive themes" ("To the Laodiceans"), which he dealt with over and over to clarify them out of disorder.

In Frost's 1935 introduction to E. A. Robinson's *King Jasper* he begins: "It may come to the notice of posterity (and then again it may not) that this, our age, ran wild in the quest of new ways to be new." After this obvious poke at Pound's "Make it new," he goes on to enumerate the ways poetry has attempted to be new. He concludes that Robinson stayed content with the "old fashioned way to be new." The old-fashioned way is more implied than stated, but we can safely assume he referred to rhyme, meter, and the traditional bag of poetic tricks the age sought to dump out and smash. But, his appreciation of Robinson does not end here. He seems to have found in Robinson something he often spoke about in his own work—"the surprise of remembering something I didn't know I knew."

So, what has this to do with the statement, made in the same essay, that a poem is "a momentary stay against confusion"? A great deal, I think. For what is a "momentary stay against confusion" but a restatement—dressed up in plain but new clothes—of the idea that art makes order out of chaos? In his own words, "All I would keep for myself is the freedom of the material—the condition of body and mind now and then to summon aptly from the vast chaos of all I have lived through."

In letters and talks Frost stresses that it is not the poet's place to startle readers with new information, to tell them what they did not know, but to have them say, along with him, that they knew that but never heard it said like that before. So, as in the poems, Frost is not seeking to say something new but to say something old in a new way— the "old fashioned way" he found in Robinson.

I mention all of this not to beg the question but to make what I think is a very important point: In prose and poetry Frost was consistent. He never veered from his belief in traditional poetic tools or from his theories of "the sound of sense" and "sentence sense." And that, I think, speaks directly to the question at hand. Though the poems may have been "momentary stay[s]," his career was a lifelong "stay." While contemporaries like Pound, Eliot, Stevens and Williams went crashing off into the unknown (chaos, confusion), Frost stood firm on older values and methods, content to let the well-made object create a quiet, still place — the small world of each poem where order reigned. This, I believe, is the "stay," what he elsewhere called "an arrest of disorder."

Every poem makes a specific, if unspoken, promise: to give the reader this "momentary stay against confusion." A sonnet, or any fixed form for that matter, makes an additional promise: to stay within recognized confines, thus taking away the element of surprise found in nonce forms, offering instead a stable, knowable pattern in which order will be established. Thus, the reader is free to follow the poem down as it melts to conclusion without consciously attending to form as well as a host of other matters.

These promises constitute a compact between poet and reader. It is understood, especially today, that the poet is allowed some leeway; but when the reader's attention is drawn more toward variations in form to such an extent that it is a distraction, then the compact is broken. Admittedly, Frost stretched the terms of the poet-reader contract with most of his sonnets, but none of the poems I have identified, and already discussed as sonnets, lead to distraction.

Chaos, not even a little bit, such as the patternless rhyme of "Mowing," can be allowed into the orderly place the poet has worked so hard to create in a world that is mostly chaos.

"Momentary," in Frost's definition of a poem, is often misinterpreted. It seems to imply a mere blip in the time continuum. But if the poem is to continue, is to be "lodged" where it might do some good, then a blip in time makes no sense. Frost was referring to space, not time. In time the poem lasts only as long as it takes to read it. In space, however, it exists always, a small, neat place to return to any time we please, a place we will always find orderly and self-contained, a "stay" against the randomness, the helter-skelter, the usual chaos of the world. So, when poems fail (as Jarrell says about a third of Frost's do), it is not only for the obvious reasons — that they are merely clever, overly quaint, cute, cracker-barrel-wishy-washy wise, etc.— but because they fail to "arrest ... disorder."

Finally, what about "confusion"? Frost had no copyright on this. An exhaustive list would take pages and would require a catalog of what baffled the people of his time, and a personal list that spanned eighty-plus years. In other words, too much for this space. Instead, it seems more prudent to look at those confusions Jarrell has called Frost's "excessive themes, those of isolation, of extinction and of the final limitations of man..." ("To the Laodiceans" 50–51). In these, I think, we find a focus that allows us to see the poem becoming organized, crafted so that confusion, chaos, disorder (call it what you will) is held at bay.

It seems appropriate here, before I examine individual poems, to mention Frost's "negative capability." Just because many of his poems ask more questions than they answer doesn't mean they don't fend off confusion. Knowing the right questions to ask is a valid method — more valid perhaps than posing tentative answers. Questions can narrow the world out of confusion, giving us a focal point where we might begin considering possible answers. Questions do not insist; hence they avoid the risk of alienating readers who do not accept the answers.

In many of the sonnets Frost deals with isolation: "The Vantage Point," "Into My Own," "A Dream Pang," "The Oven Bird," and "Acquainted with the Night" all strike me as examinations of an extreme state of being — deliberately chosen or not, real or projected. Like many of Frost's poems that deal with confusion, there is no answer to the loneliness of humanity, but an acceptance of the way things are. Human beings are isolated, but we are also empowered with guardianship, creatures with minds to know our loneliness and to seek acceptance of what "the Fall" deeded to us. The "stay" is the poem itself, the reasoned response, the working out through keen observation and the setting down in shared language of the situation, which ultimately means acceptance of it. Rilke says that the best defense is defenselessness. Acceptance is not a solution, but through it we at least arrive at a place where confusion falls away. We see the situation for what it is and find some solace in our ability to observe the details it is made of.

Frost is considered a nature poet — even though he claimed that nearly all of his poems contained people — but the nature in his poems is a means, not an end. Those who see him as a nature poet — a claim generally regarded as restrictive — are at least only half correct. Likewise, his disclaimer can be taken only half seriously. As Frost wrote in "The Secret Sits": "We dance around in a ring and suppose, / But the Secret sits in the middle and knows." Nature, then, comprises his metaphor and his synecdoche, the tools by which he examines and interprets the world.

In "The Vantage Point" the speaker has isolated himself from other men, having discovered "a slope where the cattle keep the lawn." Though hidden from other men, he can still observe them. And what he observes are the two great institutions of humanity: homes, the culmination of the urge to commune with others, to protect ourselves, and to share in the safety numbers bring; and graveyards, the place where even the dead are cared for. On the one hand, isolation may be a way to arrest the confusion brought about by living in a community. On the other hand, this pastoralism, observing human institutions from afar, may also offer a way to see again the patterns, the forms imposed on life to give it meaning and to stay the confusion that a life without laws, rules, shapes and routines would necessarily bring about. Hence, the narrator seems to say, a new vantage point can help us to refocus.

Extinction is the second theme Jarrell identifies. This observation seems correct enough in light of "Once by the Pacific" and "On a Bird Singing in Its Sleep." If not obsessive about the final downfall of humankind, Frost at least seems to have taken the prospect seriously. These two sonnets, along with many lyrics, capture the ironic nature of our existence — evolution simultaneous with devolution. As in Ovid's three eras of man — gold, silver and iron — we have evolved to a higher science but devolved to "the damned desire of having," materialism, greed, etc. Confusion? In spades. To recognize it, to state it, to fix it in space is to know it, is to control it by giving it order in the headlong, willy-nilly drive toward more.

If "On a Bird Singing in Its Sleep" is ultimately about tripping up certain demise, then "Once by the Pacific" predicts its certainty. Here, indifferent nature, following its course, simply finishes the job of covering the planet with water (a prophecy not so far off the mark given the current predictions of melting polar caps and the like). But the immediate danger observed in the power of waves is somehow moderated by further observations. The shore is "backed by cliff," the cliff by continent.

It may not be imminent danger, but it is certainly inevitable. As in the final stages of dying, with acceptance comes calm, another "stay against confusion."

I might add that here, as in "The Vantage Point," Frost chose a sonnet variant, as if to say that when the end is near we reach for the known, the acceptable, the traditional; but still we want to play with it, tweak it here and there and see what we can do to it.

Finally, limitations. This may be the most slippery of the three themes. In places Frost seems to see humanity as limitless, as in "The Master Speed." But more often we are physically limited, as in "On a Tree Fallen Across the Road," or spiritually limited, as in "Design." And there are times when acceptance of our limitations is absolutely the only way to defend ourselves against chaos.

"Design" is based on observation, but turns to resignation. Typically, Frost shrugs his shoulders after offering two equally horrible possibilities: there is nothing governing the universe, so all is random and without design, or something is governing and still allows such devil's masses to go on. Of course he can offer no answers, only questions. Answers are a matter of faith, and faith in either of these possibilities seems equally unacceptable. But what matters is this: The poem makes order out of chaos, limits the view of the situation under observation and creates another quiet (though disturbing) place where we might contemplate without distraction.

Most, but not all, of the sonnets have as part of their thematic baggage isolation, extinction or limitations. As with the poems in general, the importance of the theme varies significantly.

If each of the sonnets is an orderly house outside of which chaos thunders and storms, then Frost has built a city. The order in the houses may be disturbing, but at least the loneliness, the conflict or the fear is clear. And to identify the enemy must always be the first order of business.

Chapter 2

Into My Own

The Sonnets of *A Boy's Will*, 1913

"Into My Own"

> Originally published as "Into Mine Own" in *New England Magazine*, May 1909. Reprinted in *A Boy's Will*, 1913, and in *Complete Poems of Robert Frost*, 1968.

This poem occupies the most privileged position — the first poem in the first book — of all the poems in the Frost canon. Its position is made more important than is the case with other poets because of the unified nature of Frost's career. There were phases, of course — the sonnet period of 1906–7 and the political 1930s — but his was not a career broken down into periods or movements, like Yeats' or Eliot's, but one that built steadily one poem, one book upon the other.

It was a gamble on his part to open with a poem that boasts before there is anything to boast about, to suggest that someday he would, metaphorically, go off into the world of literary giants — "so old and firm they scarcely show the breeze" — and take his place there and not be changed. After all, Frost had met with little support in the magazines back in America. "Into My Own" had been published before its appearance in book form; however, very few of the others in the collection had. One might argue that "The Pasture" holds a position superior to "Into My Own" because, after it prefaced *North of Boston*, it was placed as the frontispiece in all the collected editions. Be that as it may, the first poem the book-reading public came in contact with in 1913 was "Into My Own." It introduced the lyrical voice that over the next fifty years was to modulate and mature but never substantially change. The poem also introduced themes, subjects, attitudes and Frost's tendency toward self-absorption, all of which were as firmly planted then as they would ever be.

It is a rebellious poem from a rebellious poet. It is a beacon announcing that the poet who speaks here will speak against tradition while speaking from deep within it. And, as is typical in Frost, he can and does have it both ways. In Frost the feat of holding opposites in the mind at the same time occurs often, not only in this book but throughout the eight additional collections he would publish. In one sense, the poem is no less an announcement of a revolution than was Wordsworth's "Preface" to *Lyrical Ballads*. It is the "Preface," sans the rhetoric and the lengthy justifications. The poem announces in its overt message, as well as in its form, that it will not be traveling the well-worn highway, that it will, in fact, cut a new road to where the pioneer might live comfortably away from others, both physically and artistically. Simultaneously, Frost blends two well-established forms — sonnet and couplet — to create a true hybrid — sacrificing both and neither for something greater just as deftly as he'd blended his farming and writing lives, a hermit's existence at Derry with the desire always to reach a vast audience. These conflicting notions are set forth here for the first, but hardly the last, time.

The poem also makes another major announcement: that Frost is going to experiment, not by blasting conventions and traditions as his contemporaries were doing, but by working within the tradition. In 1931, Thompson reports, Frost wrote to Louis Untermeyer, saying, "I started calling myself a Synecdochist when others called themselves Imagists or Vorticists. Always, always a larger significance. A little thing touches a larger thing" (*Years of Triumph* 693). This statement is significant because it can also be taken as a comment on his use of the sonnet, the form that most specifically represents tradition in his work. Hence, to respect the sonnet is to respect the tradition.

In one very real sense he is mounting a full-blown attack on one of the bastions of poetry, the sonnet, and he is doing so in reverence for the form rather than in contempt for it. Although he may, from the very beginning, think he is "pretending" these lyrics are not sonnets, they very obviously parade the form before the reader, as if to say: "See how the traditional holds up under attack? See how it will bend, but not break?" Granted, "Into My Own" does not test the form to its limits as others of his sonnets do, but for a poem written by an American poet in the early 1900s, it very nearly bursts the limits — at least in comparison to what his contemporaries (except Robinson) were doing. Frost was no provincial rube blundering along, testing himself and, coincidentally, the sonnet form on the way. Frost's Derry sonnets, and all the sonnets that followed, were experiments calculated to discover just how far the poet could stray, and the form could flex, to accommodate each other — "the poem begins in delight and ends in wisdom, the figure is the same for love" — he would later write, and like true lovers the poet and his lover/form test each other. Each tentative, delightful beginning eventually yields some new insight, some new wisdom as the poet and form face off for a dance or a wrestling match. The figure changes from poem to poem.

"Into My Own" is a projection of what might be. It is a threat, perhaps, to some, a promise, perhaps, to himself—"One of my wishes is..."—but it is not a description of what is. Later in his life Frost would write to Louis Untermeyer about "The Road Not Taken" that he was "fooling myself along...." The poem constantly hedges, as "The Road Not Taken" does, and many of his great lyrics do also, and never commits; it questions but offers no, or only tentative, answers — Keats' "negative capability"? "I should not be withheld...," "I do not see why...," "They would not find me...." It is the great "What if." What if I were to move away from civilization? What if I were to shun the society of men? What if I were to depend solely on myself? The poem answers those questions only generally, vaguely: they would find me more certain of who I have always been.

Within *A Boy's Will* a second sonnet also finds the poet estranged — this time from a wife/lover in a dream — and a third sonnet reveals him finally, if only momentarily, detached from social encumbrances. But in "Into My Own" it is mere speculation, a pure "what if" situation that offers an answer based utterly on that speculation: regardless of where I go, how far I go, and for how long I go, I will always be who I am now — perhaps more so! Is this a conservative attitude, or a strong sense of self? Whatever, it proved a truism. By *In the Clearing* there was little change in the attitude, the posture, and the tone from *A Boy's Will*. As early as 1926 Frost wrote to Bernard De Voto: "Any decent philosophy and all philosophy has to [be] static. Else what would there be to distinguish it from science? ... My philosophy ... I hold more or less unbroken from youth to age" (*Later Years* 21).

"Into My Own" is a poem full of bravado and a self-assuredness that implies the "Boy" of the title is merely a mask for the man-poet who has lived the life and now reports on that life at thirty-eight years of age. All of the poems in *A Boy's Will* are personal lyrics, and the gloss that appeared for each one in the first edition gave Frost some objective distance. They removed him from direct confession and allowed him to stand back, observe and organize the poems into a larger statement. All of the poems are, of course, very early work, but the best are already mature, and "Into My Own" stands among those. If there is a boy seeking to escape and test himself against the world, there is a man beside him restraining him, assuring him that escape is not going away from people but being an individual among them and being certain of his identity in the process. Other poems do find the persona distanced from his kind, but "Into My Own" is simply a first tentative, speculative and imaginative step outward from the crowd.

"Into My Own" is connected to "Once by the Pacific" in its use of couplets and by its speculative/prophetic nature. As Frost's books built a larger and more complex worldview, the 1928 "Once by the Pacific" seems to look back over its shoulder for some reassurance about its ability to prophesy in light of the earlier "Into My Own." And certainly by 1928 the tentative, speculative poet of the earlier work could be seen as an accurate forecaster, for by then Frost was a loner among loners, at a distance from his fellow poets, and, we see now, "...more sure of all [he] thought was true."

"On a Bird Singing in Its Sleep" is also written in couplets and likewise bears more than a structural resemblance to "Into My Own." Characters in both poems are self-protective, and both poems concern survival—figuratively and literally. The human character blusters, and the bird merely peeps, but both utter defiance at a potentially hostile world. And both, it should not be forgotten, do it within a double poetic/musical context of couplet and sonnet.

Despite the experimentation with couplets, "Into My Own" displays an obviously heavy debt to the English sonnet. The quatrains provide the first visual evidence that the poem will test the sonnet form by utilizing couplets, a form that has nearly the same historical significance as the sonnet. The quatrains subsume the couplets by turning each stanza into a syntactical unit. In essence this makes each reliant upon the other and negates any sense of dominance. Hence, by blending the two stanza forms, he has created a new one, at least within the context of the sonnet.

The insistent "Is" of stanzas one through three establish the norm that the turn must break. And, as elegantly as any turn in Frost's sonnets, this one does so by gracefully turning the poem over to "they." Emphatically, epigrammatically, the poem concludes by subtly placing a kind of burden on the "other"—society, other artists?—those, the closing couplet seems to suggest, who made him want to leave in the first place, who forced him to test himself against some great nonhuman entity or against himself or ultimately against the poetic tradition.

And in a brash, almost insolent, closing line he reports that the urge they created in him to run away has backfired on them, and he is as self-confident as ever.

The stalwart, unbending dark trees of the first couplet look suspiciously like the nineteenth-century poets and traditions that Frost and Robinson are sometimes accused of resurrecting. If those traditions were so powerful for Frost, why then would we be confronted with "gloom" and "doom" in the second couplet? The stanza states that the speaker wishes that they weren't gloom and doom, but, alas, they in fact are. It is a complicated, almost ambiguous sentence, but it appears to say: "I wish these big, dark woods were not a pretty, inviting disguise for melancholy and pessimism. I wish they merely led up to death and destruction's front door — then stopped. But they are a disguise, and they do harbor doom." Consequently, the next two stanzas boldly predict that he will "some day" escape into them and be content to stay, and others, who still care about him, should be encouraged to track him down to check on his well-being. But there is no actual motion into the woods; they invite, he considers their invitation, and withholds an ultimate decision in very nearly the pattern of invitation/consideration/rejection that Robert Penn Warren discusses in his essay "The Themes of Robert Frost." And ultimately, withholding a decision, merely predicting it, constitutes the final rejection part of the triad.

What makes this poem slippery is the underlying cause for his desire to "steal away." It is not overtly stated, and it only tentatively suggests that others are the cause. Running away, or escaping, is a theme that occurs over and over again in Frost. But if the poem is taken, as I first suggested, not as an escape but as a boast that he will someday join the nineteenth-century greats of American literature, then his inclination to move on is clear. In either case, be it boast, threat or promise, we have a poem that clearly lays out directions and themes and tensions that he will continue to explore over and over for the next half century.

Frost was a master prosodist and he often established subtexts, via substitutions, that are as telling and ingenious as any other aspect of the poem — theme, tension or technique.

The opening line begins with a trochee and ends on a spondee. The medial foot is pyrrhic. In other words, these attributes create an atypically irregular line for Frost. However, if we take this stanza to be an allusion to the nineteenth-century masters, then the line, as it falters, may simply be setting us up for the second line, which is as regular as the first is irregular, and certainly offers us a prosodic model Frost would have partly caught from them. Most of the six spondees and four trochees in the poem — the predominant variations — form a gloss of the poem if they are taken together: "dark trees," "I should," "some day," "Fearless," "wheel pours," "turn back," "set forth," "more sure."

The syntactical parallelism of "I should not" and "I do not" only strengthens the turn at "They would not...." Likewise, the five "shoulds," showing contingency or probability (depending upon the reading) strengthen the resignation couched in the boast or threat and the tentativeness of the threat. Furthermore, the five occurrences of "not" create a strong, negative undercurrent that reinforces the tone of the entire poem. The persona somehow appears to stand firm even when he is most obviously hedging on his commitment. Again, this is typical Frost, pitting opposites against one another as he builds toward a third, and completely individual position built on, but apart from, the other two.

"A Dream Pang"

> According to Lawrance Thompson, "the earliest known manuscript" of this poem appears in a letter to Susan Hayes Ward on August 6, 1907. A note stated, "I shall master the sonnet form in time." Published in *A Boy's Will*, 1913, and reprinted in *Complete Poems of Robert Frost*, 1968.

"A Dream Pang" is packed with irony. To see the poem on the page prompts one to assume that it is purely Italian in structure. It has a clear octave rhymed *abbaabba* that is separated from a sestet that also begins Italian, but concludes on an English couplet. The poem also creates the illusion that it is turning on line nine. But that is only an illusion. The octave is a single syntactical unit. At the stanza break between lines eight and nine, a new syntactical unit begins, thus creating the sense that the poem turns. The illusion is helped along by the negative "not," but we quickly discover that the "not" of line nine is the same "not" of lines five and seven. The new sentence seems as if it is about to tell us something new, but it merely restates what we already knew, that the poet was standing close to his wife, albeit hidden from her. Lines nine through twelve create a second syntactical unit and the couplet a third. The actual turn occurs at line thirteen, and it is a very English epigrammatical close. So, rather than a strict Italian sonnet, we have yet another hybrid. Although this poem is hardly as experimental as "Into My Own," it still very obviously tampers with the reader's expectations of a sonnet, just as it tampers with other expectations that *A Boy's Will* has established.

A Boy's Will toys with the idea of escape. From the boast/threat/promise to escape/run away in "Into My Own," the poems have moved steadily into more isolation. Yet "A Dream Pang" is only a dream of isolation. In reality the persona's partner could not be much more intimately situated. He is relating the dream as he wakes in bed with her. Distance is implied because of the content of the dream, but with brief, strategic stage direction it is made very clear that the speaker did not dream the partner coming to the edge of his woods but had dreamed the partner coming to the edge of the dreamed woods. Miss the parenthetical remark in line four and you have a very different reading of the poem.

A third irony appears in the speaker's willingness to communicate when communication is least possible and his inability to "call" when communication might make a difference. The psychological distance this opens up between the two characters is ultimately the most real distance in the poem. In lines one and two the speaker tells us "my song / Was swallowed up in leaves that blew away." A fragile song, indeed, and a song that has been wasted on all but the singer. Perhaps this is a way of saying that the song is lost without the partner to hear it, but what then do we make of line eleven: "And the sweet pang it cost me not to call?" This certainly underscores the persona's ambivalent feelings in the dream situation. Yet, on waking, he immediately tells his partner of the dream. Again, we are witness to Frost holding opposites in mind simultaneously.

This is a poem, too, of tensions between opposites. Dream and reality, lost words and lost chances have already been discussed. But there are also here opposing characters. She is characterized by words such as "ponder" and "pensive," whereas the dominant impression of the speaker is of one who physically runs away after doing harm. Thompson suggests that Frost may have written the poem for Elinor as a way to apologize for some real or imagined wrong he committed. But regardless of the impetus for the poem, it remains, clearly, a love poem. Beyond that, the poem establishes that there is, in fact, a place to come home to after the running away is finished. It also presages the poet's return to people at the end of *A Boy's Will* and in *North of Boston*, Frost's "book of people."

For all but the closing couplet, "A Dream Pang" is a dark poem filled with negatives — "not" appears five times — and words that imply negation — "withdrawn," "swallowed up," "blown away," "stray" and "wrong." Even the couplet resolves on a positive note that began on a negative one. In this aspect "A Dream Pang" and "Into My Own" are intimately connected. "Into My Own" also contains five uses of the word "not" and a basketful of words connoting negativity. Too, the projected action of "Into My Own" has now been accomplished in "A Dream Pang" — if only in a sleeping state. The speaker's resolve to run away in the first poem now seems to puzzle him in the second after it has, at least figuratively, happened. The effect is somewhat disarming, but the poems were certainly not written to complement one another. To paraphrase James M. Cox, the poems were not written to finish out books, but the books were created from finished poems (quoted in Cook 336).

"A Dream Pang" also seems to anticipate "The Oven Bird" (probably written about the same time, 1900–1910 at Derry) in that the "singers" in both poems are "diminished things." If the oven bird has reduced itself in order to survive, the persona here seems to have failed, or at least diminished himself, out of pure stubbornness. The bird "frames" his question "in all but words," and the speaker in "A Dream Pang" has had his song "blown away" and later will not speak, even though he has ample chance. Either way, diminished is diminished, and each singer is left to deal with himself and the world in whatever ways left to him.

We must remember also that the walker in "Acquainted with the Night" drops his eyes as he passes the watchman, "unwilling to explain." The bird in "On a Bird Singing in Its Sleep" utters half a song and then is still out of self-protection. The birds in "Never Again Would Bird's Song Be the Same" have picked up an "oversound, / Her tone of meaning but without the words." In all of these cases there is partial or aborted or refused communication, a limitation that seems to be partly compensated for by the use of the sonnet form, which carries with it conventions and traditions that can contribute to understanding even when words themselves fail.

Whereas "A Dream Pang" is an apology, "The Oven Bird" apologizes for nothing, accepting the very real need to survive in inhospitable environments no matter what. And in that sense the two poems differ greatly. "A Dream Pang" deals with human estrangement; "The Oven Bird" deals with estrangement from the world for the sake of solitude and escape from the "dust" of human inventions.

Although "A Dream Pang" is not of uppermost importance among the sonnets, it does provide a transition from the threat/promise posture of "Into My Own" to the actual separation from people in "The Vantage Point." ("A Dream Pang" is the fifteenth poem in the volume, "The Vantage Point" seventeenth.) Furthermore it introduces the male/female, husband/wife conflicts and relationships that would be featured so prominently in *North of Boston* and beyond.

"The Vantage Point"

> Curiously little is written about the history of this poem anywhere. Thompson never mentions it in his three-volume biography. First published (apparently) in *A Boy's Will*, 1913, and reprinted in *Complete Poems of Robert Frost*, 1968.

"The Vantage Point" has not been widely written about, but when it is discussed it is often in superlatives, especially with regard to the technical mastery. A reading of Paul Fussell's treatment of the poem is necessary for a true appreciation of Frost's metrical skills, most specifically with the turn in the sonnet.

Although Frost stated his preference for both Shakespearean and Wordsworthian sonnets, this is the only poem that borrows from the Wordsworthian rhyme scheme. The *abbaacca* of the octave is accurate, but the sestet is pure Frostian invention. The strict form would have called for four rhymes—*cddccd* or *cdcddc* (or five in one version, *cddece*—but here Frost uses six: *deedff*.

Like the strictness of the form in the octave, the subject too is conventional and finally introduces us, in a sonnet, to the theme of escape that shapes *A Boy's Will*. Even though I won't return to the world of men, he tells us, I will go and look at them, or at least at their institutions—white houses and churches for the living, well-kept graves for the dead. This places him, then, somewhere in between. He is not a true member of society because he has run away from it, yet he is not clinically dead. So, as a privileged observer, he can choose his vantage point daily to observe people, comment on them or turn away from it all as he pleases.

Line five is a small study in contrasts, both in image and in language: "Myself unseen, I see in white refined...." The "unseen/see" pattern is one that Frost uses often throughout his poems. At times he pits a word against its negative, or a negative variant as he does here, and at others he places the same form of the word in different relationships to the sentence or a single image. In "The Mountain" Frost uses this device more often perhaps than in any other single poem. Words seem to echo like the returning voice in "The Most of It" back from the mountain. It gives an eerie quality to the lines and demands a reader's very close attention. At times he appears to contradict himself but really does not. At other times he does contradict himself, though he appears not to—as he does so brilliantly in "The Road Not Taken," fooling every generation of valedictorians since the poem first appeared.

"I see in white defined" is very nearly a gloss for his most famous sonnet, "Design," originally entitled "In White." The contrast implied by the line, that the background must be dark, is certainly a visual doubling of the light/dark dyad of the next two lines that image the two great human institutions, earthly home (house) and eternal home (grave) against ultimate darkness of death and/or unknowing. The "farther" of line six makes it clear that he is talking about actual distance, not figurative distance. The graves are behind the house; they don't just follow the houses as homes.

"The Vantage Point" at last offers us a character who has escaped the world of men, at least to the extent that from this distant hillside he can observe without being observed. In "Into My Own" he says he will someday escape, and that escape implies a kind of power. In "A Love Pang" he escapes in the course of a dream, but he has no real power because all is controlled by the dream. Here at last the themes of escape and the resulting power are both fulfilled. The detached observation of the octave gives way to a more intimate sestet where the persona can, when he is tired of watching men and women go about their lives, "turn" — both physically on his arm, and figuratively in the poem — to matters more immediate and to matters controllable by the speaker.

He first pivots so that the sunburned hillside begins to burn his face. From this point the speaker and the poem pick up speed toward an ever-narrowing, yet ever-expanding, world and experience: his breathing "shakes the bluet like a breeze, / I smell the earth, I smell the bruisèd plant." And finally, "I look into the crater of an ant." The images pick up magnitude also as they rush toward closure and ultimately leave the reader hanging with no closure at all. In a few brief lines we have moved from a man overwhelmed by, and hence escaped from, the world, to one who envisions himself in an *Alice in Wonderland* relationship with the ant hole he discovers beside him after his "turn." Although size and relationship shift — he at once shakes the flowers with a breath and confronts a hyperbolized chasm — the speaker is growing, making new connections and being forced to reconsider himself in light of these new relationships.

Frost has said that "the most exciting movement in nature is not progress, advance, but expansion and contraction," and the end of "The Vantage Point" certainly seems written to illustrate the definition, or the definition written to explain the poem. But breathe this sestet does: expanding to change relationship to the hillside, contracting as breath shakes the flowers, expanding wide to smell the universal (earth), contracting to smell the local (bruisèd plant). The final line is curious for being either expansion *or* contraction. If he contracts and looks into the ant hole as an ant, the "crater" (typically a large depression) makes sense. And, if he expands and moves human-sized even closer to the hole, then there, too, "crater" makes sense as he zooms in, the tiny writ large in this new proximity. The changing relationships are dizzying in their speed. The octave has moved slowly, almost in geological time, the slow motion of historical observation.

But as the distance between observer and observed shortens in the sestet, time seems to speed up, and that which is brought closer to the eye suddenly takes on the ability to confuse or create appearances that expand and contract, dilate and shrink. There is a kind of heavy, deep breathing here that seems only to quicken even as it expands itself in a final rush of images.

The leisurely pace of the opening two lines of the sestet are masterful in their ability to establish expectation and then to whip that expectation headlong into a frenzy of observations led by a series of "I" clauses that dazzle and can't but wear themselves out in an exhaustion that sucks all of the air out of that small space. Although "The Vantage Point" does not close in any conventional manner, it does, again in typical Frost style, find a way to end originally, organically and without seeming to do anything out of the ordinary.

This ability to make the "seem" dominate what is actually happening in a poem is what so eluded early critics who wrote Frost off as a mere New England poet of woodland scenes. It is also what has captivated later critics as the appearance of simplicity has slowly been peeled away, and the complicated dualities discovered. Frost signaled some firm directions and practices in *A Boy's Will*.

Chapter 3

Range-Finding

The Sonnets of *Mountain Interval,* 1916

3 : The Sonnets of *Mountain Interval*, 1916

Anyone familiar with the Lawrance Thompson biography of Frost, or with William Pritchard's praiseworthy attempt in *Robert Frost: A Literary Life Reconsidered* to correct some of Thompson's aggressions toward Frost, is probably well aware that Frost wrote at least twelve of the thirty poems in *Mountain Interval* during the same period of time as the poems in *A Boy's Will* and *North of Boston*. All of the poems identified in this book as sonnets were composed, according to Thompson, in 1906–1907, a period he calls Frost's sonnet period. It should be noted that a number of poems that look like sonnets, and are often called sonnets, also originated during this time—"Mowing," "Hyla Brook" and "A Line Gang" most notably. Thompson goes so far as to identify these poems specifically as sonnets despite their lengths and extreme departures from rhyme conventions.

"Meeting and Passing"

>Published in *Mountain Interval*, 1916, and reprinted in *Complete Poems of Robert Frost*, 1968.

"Meeting and Passing" may have its genesis in the same time period as the sonnets of *A Boy's Will*, but it is different. Rather than the sought-for estrangement of those poems, this one literally yearns for closeness and acceptance. The two characters are moving in opposite directions. And even though they only "mingle great and small / Footprints in summer dust," they have made contact, and from that point, the poem suggests, there will be more significance to the fact that they enter, after parting, a space previously occupied by the other; in other words, they share each other's "past." And because the meeting, innocent as it may have been, was tinged with very obvious sexual overtones, the suggestion appears to be that the two part closer than before. The inevitable has been set into motion — marriage. And this is no small point, as Frost was one of the great poets of marriage.

Her parasol "thrust[s]" "the decimal" in the dust. That she is performing this action is significant. She is maintaining the distance between them. And not only that, there is a vast difference between "a" decimal, which we might have expected, and "the" decimal, which is decidedly stronger, and what he wrote.

It is also interesting that Frost chose the language of math here — a language devoid of connotations, though he playfully attempts to give them some — using "decimal" instead of "period," since a decimal divides and a period brings to a full stop. And he had the option to use either because the word "figure" two lines before could be either a numerical figure or a linguistic one. The playfulness of "less than two / But more than one" quite clearly imitates the up/down motion of the two walkers. That is to say, there is a kind of shuffling motion throughout the poem — in the opposing directions the two characters walk in, in the parry and thrust of their awkward conversation, in the doubletalk of the numbers and finally in their inability to make eye contact. Social intercourse, then, is taken about as far, figuratively, towards sexual intercourse as the times and the poet would permit. Frost is a poet of great subtlety, a fact missed by critics for many years and dismissed by others for years after that. But once readers discover this kind of "play" in the poems, they will also find that it abounds. Whereas Frost's poems were once dismissed as overly simple, they are now often cited for their unnerving delicacy. The sexuality here is but one example.

This up-and-down, back-and-forth, or shuffling motion also suggests the myth of Sisyphus, that poor mythical character doomed to an eternity of pushing a boulder up a hill only to have it roll back down again. But Sisyphus was also known as a trickster, and it may be that Frost identified with him, at least to the extent that Frost, too, could be sly of tongue.

In 1895 Frost wanted desperately to marry Elinor; in fact, he had been waiting none too patiently since they graduated from high school in 1892. Elinor was attending St. Lawrence University on an accelerated four-years-in-three track, but even that was too long for Frost. "Meeting and Passing," written some years after the actual events to commemorate that summer, carries with it a sense of desperation — controlled and objectified at this point in time, long after they were married, but that distance between them still seems palpable — and the choice of the up/down, back-and-forth motion in the poem, the unsteadiness, definitely underscores a sense of despair. On the surface the poet appears to be resigned to the situation, but there is no denying the telltale imagery. In Randall Jarrell's words the closing lines are "the transfiguring, almost inexpressible reaching out of the self to what has become closer and more personal than self" (60).

As with so many of Frost's poems, the very manipulation of the form is yet another comment on the action or the situation. Here the conventions of courtship are held up to the mirror of sonnet conventions. The poem begins regularly enough with an Italian (*abbaabba*) octave, but it concludes on a typical Frost variation, employing an English couplet (itself a variant here, as a word cannot rhyme with itself.) The poem seems to suggest that things begin conventionally enough: meeting accidentally, talking, being coy or timid. But the unconventional sestet suggests that the rest of this courtship will not follow all the rules. If Thompson is to be believed (and he is usually very reliable with these kinds of facts), then the sonnet documents an event or a compressed series of events that took place between Frost and Elinor White (the future Mrs. Frost) at Ossipee Mountain in 1895. And the history of the Frost/White courtship was anything but fairytale-like or conventional.

A manipulator of the sonnet form, Frost likewise is a master prosodist, carefully substituting spondees — most significant here — and forcing readers to listen very carefully to the subtext he is creating in these feet. In line three there are two spondees — "just turned" and "saw you" — followed in the next line by "We met," perhaps the shortest sentence in the entire canon. If that were all of the spondaic substitutions, we would still have the poem in miniature. But that is not all. "Footprints," in line six is certainly central to the imagery of the poem on a number of levels, as is "deep thrust" in line nine. "Down there" in line eleven literally refers to the dust at her feet, but down there is where he is headed, "down the hill," through her past, as it were, merely dust compared to what the future holds for him.

Almost as deft as the turn in "The Vantage Point," the turn here is absolute, and it not only delineates between the two parts of the sonnet, but it places a mark, "the decimal," squarely between the man and the woman, leaving no doubt that there is still distance between them. Perhaps that distance is not as permanent as a period would suggest, but certainly it is more concrete than the young Robert Frost might have hoped for. The suggestion, at least, is that that decimal is as strong and inhibiting as the wall we met in the opening line.

Given Frost's penchant for walls and barriers of all types, it is interesting that he did not place his characters on either side of the wall or even on either side of the gate. They remain on the same side, but they are unable to cross something as insignificant as a point in the dust. Again, Frost's sense of helplessness at this point in his life in regard to Elinor seems to be captured in this image. Even if there were no biographical facts to support such a reading, the fact remains that something tiny is often the stumbling block to happiness. There is a whole life of loneliness and isolation packed into that decimal point.

"The Oven Bird"

> Published in *Mountain Interval*, 1916, and reprinted in *Complete Poems of Robert Frost*, 1968.

In his biography of Frost, William Pritchard tells the story of Sidney Cox, a student of Frost's, perusing *Mountain Interval* then writing to Frost addressing him as "Dear Oven Bird," rather than "Mr. Frost." Cox believed that he had discovered a "key" to understanding Frost. However, Frost insisted that Cox made too much of the poem and dismissed his praise and his insight. But Pritchard suggests that Cox was indeed on to something, that perhaps this was one of the doors in the poems that Frost spoke of but one not secured fast enough, leaving the student the opportunity to view the master unguarded where it was left ajar.

And such an interpretation seems fair enough. "What he frames in all but words" is certainly tantalizingly close to "the sound of sense" theory Frost developed. On any number of levels, according to the biographies, Frost felt himself to be a "diminished thing." As Cox rightly pointed out, Frost's voice was not loud, but it had been heard — if not by "everyone" then at least by a significant number of important listeners. And Frost the popularizer was certainly at work making sure his poems and books were read — if not at the time the poems were written, then when they were published ten or more years later.

In that regard it is worth suggesting that this poem, written in the same period as the sonnets of *A Boy's Will*, perhaps takes up an image introduced in "Into My Own," that of the trees, metaphorically the solid poetic giants of the nineteenth century whom Frost admired and boasted/threatened/promised to move among in that poem. If that is the case, then the speaker in "The Oven Bird" has achieved that distinction, at least in his own mind, when he says, "Who makes the solid tree trunks sound again."

I don't think it is much of a stretch to say that a number of Frost's poems were prophetic. His Swedenborgian mother was convinced she was gifted with second sight, and she believed the same about her son. Hence, if this is a poem that projects itself into the future, then the poet had again predicted where he would be several years after the poem was written—a widely read, popular poet whose publisher pushed him to get *Mountain Interval* ready for publication very shortly after the American publication of *A Boy's Will* and *North of Boston*. Yes, he was a singer people had heard, and yes he was middle-aged, and yes in singing he knew not to sing (just as the "sound of sense" and "sentence sense" demanded).

But more importantly, and what early critics chronically passed over, is the inherent social criticism and the spiritual angst suggested by the line, "He says the highway dust is over all." There is in that line a complaint that not only the highway, a construction of man's, but the machines those highways were designed for, diminish our contact with nature, with the world. And there is a question: Have our inventions improved our place in the world, or more likely, what are we to make of our reduced station?

What we have then are two distinct poems or two very different readings of one poem—two ways of saying one thing in terms of another. Ostensibly the sonnet is about a bird, a teacher bird (another name for it), and its song that is no song at all but a jumble of notes concluding with *teacher teacher*, which makes it distinct from other birds. The diminished thing is himself or the world immediately around him, the season, what have you.

A personal reading of the poem says it is about the poet, as Cox saw it, the singer who has craftily, modernistically, learned to avoid the obvious eccentricities and pomposities of the nineteenth century and to use the sound of everyday speech; hence he has learned "in singing not to sing." The poet views the world around him, his own arrival at middle age, the diminution of the beauty of youth that comes during the blink of an eye, "a moment overcast." He has, finally, achieved the escape that played so heavily in *A Boy's Will*, and in a sense has avoided some of the "highway dust" that coats the world — but not completely, for it "is over all." The diminished thing is himself, his own life. At about the time of the publication of *Mountain Interval* he confided in Louis Untermeyer, perhaps only half teasingly, that the poet in him had died ten years before. This was an exaggeration, to be sure, but it does give credence to the reading of the final line as being a reference to himself, as well as his own beliefs about himself and perhaps his poetic powers.

Finally, it is a poem that is huge with philosophical despair and doubt. It is a poem that compresses all of his "obsessive themes" into fourteen lines — isolation, extinction, and human limitations. The bird almost blusters in the face of these concerns. It is reminiscent of Virginia Woolf's moth kicking at death, hopeless and helpless but not giving up. There is a sense, despite the bravado of the opening lines (a bravado like that exhibited in "Into My Own"), that all has gone to smash, for every image that follows is a negative one — the "petal-fall," the "moment overcast," the "highway dust," the nonsinging, and the "diminished thing." This is grief so deep and absolute that we have to wonder at the strength it took to write the poem at all.

It is not at all unusual to find this kind of "confusion" addressed and "arrested" in Frost, fixed to the page and hence to the mind like pins through a butterfly's wings. But what is so striking is how very long it takes for the depth of the pain to make itself known. The true sense of pain and desperation is elusive because the very form on the page, the very act of creating that form, is often enough to "stay" or "arrest" the confusion sufficiently to make it appear as if there is no confusion at all — and never was. It is only when we realize that what "He says" is the persona translating what he wants the bird to say that we realize that the speaker is externalizing his own dark mood through the bird as certainly as Hardy does through his "Darkling Thrush" or Whitman through his widowed "he-bird."

Yet here is another stumbling block: in choosing to write the poem, in other words "to sing," in a very strict form, he has done precisely what he says he knows not to do, and hasn't done. Again, the very subtlety, the illusion and the reality demand absolute attention to every word on the page, and a healthy skepticism when we are told *anything*. To take anything we are told in the poem at face value is no way to approach Frost, who believed absolutely that the poem was a way "to say one thing in terms of another." From the very first line we should be on guard. No absolutes can be trusted — not "everyone" has heard the oven bird. From there on it is nip and tuck as the poet gains his wisdom as the poem builds. And it is one hell of a ride, one that insists that we climb back to the top and do it again, for in rereading the poem down we see what we missed each time before.

It is not surprising that Frost is again "not artless" in his prosody. A cursory look at the rhyme scheme of "The Oven Bird" seems to reveal patternless rhyming to rival that of "Mowing" — which would make this too a great poem but not a sonnet. But a closer look shows us indeed an intricate pattern: He opens with a couplet *aa*, followed by *bcb* which he links, via the medial rhyme, with the next three lines *dcd*. While rhyme links these two line groupings, the couplet is locked to the *bcb* syntactically; the first *b* rhyme is the last line of the first sentence. The *cb* lines that follow are a sentence themselves. The next lines, *dcd*, are, as I said, linked to the previous lines via rhyme. They are also linked to the couplet *ff* by yet another syntactical connection. The second couplet's function, like the *aa* couplet, is to introduce us to something: *aa* introduces us to the bird, *ff* introduces us to two great human failures — the biblical "Fall" in the first line and the failure of the human technological experiment in the second. This is the place in the poem where the human persona is most obvious, and human concerns are spoken of in human terms, not through the bird's interpreted speech. The turn, such as it is, appears to occur after line ten when we return to the bird being spoken about as it was in the opening lines. In what turns out to be another tour de force, Frost insists that we return to the beginning of the poem, that we see the interconnectedness of things by using a rhyme pair that strongly echoes the introductory couplet. I doubt that one could find another sonnet as intricately and subtly designed as this one.

Of course, for most poets, such a display of technical brilliance would be enough. But Frost is not content to stop here, nor is he undesigning in putting one final, subtle demonstration of the diminution he talks openly about in the closing two lines: according to at least one scansion both of those lines are, themselves, diminished, at least in terms of the form. Both lines contain only four stresses, not the requisite five. In line thirteen only the first syllable of "question," "frames," "all," and "words" can possibly call for stresses. "That," which by its placement would seem to take stress is passed over, in any reading, much too quickly. At best it might take a light secondary stress. Thus, there is a very loose iambic, but it gives the impression of being a four-stress line.

The final line deserves its own space for discussion. Although the line is pentameter, and it begins with two iambic feet, it is the cause of an illusion. "Of a," medially, may be another pyrrhic. However, the line can also be scanned as two iambs followed by two anapests. Either way, two iambs followed by two anapests, or two iambs followed by a pyrrhic and two more iambs, there is a four stress line, a final technical burst after most of the crowd has turned away, another masterful stroke that once more demonstrates the need to pay absolute attention to every aspect of every poem, for none goes unmanipulated and uncontrolled down to the merest minim.

"Putting in the Seed"

> Originally published in England in *Poetry and Drama*, December 1914. Reprinted in *Mountain Interval*, 1916, and reprinted in *Complete Poems of Robert Frost*, 1968.

"Putting in the Seed" is a largely unacknowledged Frost masterpiece that should replace a number of his anthology poems that simply do not hold a candle to it. This poem comes as close as any of his I can think of to fulfilling many of his definitions of what a poem is and what it should do: it is playful, sensuous, a clear "stay against confusion," and it "melts" to conclusion with nods to both the Shakespearean and Spenserian rhyme schemes, although it ultimately creates one purely its own. It is a poem prosodically firm in the tradition yet with a twist that makes it all Frost. It is thematically within the tradition as well, but again its deceptively simple treatment of "country" subject matter contains a sly wink. Clearly, Frost is having one hell of a good time here.

It really does not come as any surprise that this poem is not well

3 : The Sonnets of *Mountain Interval*, 1916

known, for it neither contributes to nor perpetuates the "other" character that Frost himself helped create. It is rural, it is seemingly simple in both subject and form, and it contains the more familiar Frost images of planting/harvesting, fallen apple blossoms, a husband and wife communicating. And these things are comforting because they are familiar and nonthreatening. But it is much more blatantly sensual and sexual than any of the other sonnets that contain that theme ("Meeting and Passing," for example).

Perhaps only the poem "The Subverted Flower" comes as close to a statement of sexual desire or longing as this one does.

The poem has at least two distinct readings. Both offer very different results. A straightforward present-tense reading, wherein the speaker is addressing his wife who has come to fetch him to dinner, is perhaps the most obvious. But it seems more likely that Frost would have used the perfect tense — "You've" — if he had wanted the reader to place the action at the time it was happening. The shift to the contraction would have had no effect on the meter and it would have made absolutely clear what time of day it is. But, of course, that is not what he wrote.

Just as it is with so many of Frost's poems, what appears to be happening is far from what really is. The subtle, everyday speech seduces us into believing we stand firmly in one place: here, in a field with a farmer burying apple blossoms as compost with his bean and pea seeds. But we look more closely and discover that in fact we may not be in that field, nor has anything alluded to taken place yet. We do not know where we are — in a kitchen, on a porch, in a bedroom as the farmer heads out to work for the day? We do not know, cannot know, because we have not been told. What we do know is this: the farmer, addressing, presumably, his wife, asks her to come and fetch him when dinner is ready. The rest is merely what he projects he will be doing when she arrives.

The poem is a challenge to her not to become like her husband, "Slave to a springtime passion for the earth." And in that challenge is a charge, too, to resist the sexual urges implied by that passion and given voice in the next line, "How Love burns through the Putting in the Seed" — if she can. With its out-of-place capitalizations it is hard to miss the double intentions of the lines. But that aside, what are we to make of this projection of labor that looks so tantalizingly like the act itself? After all, "the act is the sweetest dream that labor knows," not the projection of act, which is passive. Is this, then, a negation of the earlier statement? Is this part of the "play" that Frost was so fond of? The poem certainly plants questions like seeds that demand birth into answers.

It is well known that many of Frost's poems are directed to Elinor. Whether they are occasioned by arguments, or are simply expressions of his desire to have the two of them pitted against the world — together, alone — this is serious play, an invitation to abandon the world for a while, to ignore obligations and simply enjoy the spring, passion and, by extension, perhaps physical love. Like the little poem "The Pasture" that first appeared in *North of Boston*, there is a clear dare presented. In the earlier poem it is "You come too." Here, in "Putting in the Seed," it is echoed by "You come to..." If it were not for Frost's well-known gamesmanship, such a phrase could be written off as coincidence, but the similarity, the resonance between the two, leaves little thought that this was a matter of chance. Frost may have waited for the poems to come to him, but once they did he was a masterful manipulator of their power and meaning, not only as they applied within the poem and the book but within the growing canon.

The poem begins with the speaker giving directions to his wife, shifts to what he will be doing when she arrives, makes a parenthetical aside concerning the potency of the petals when buried with seeds, then very casually shifts focus to the wife and quickly to the two of them "mingled" like the earlier pea and bean seeds. And that is where the couple is left at the end of this nine-line octave, together, and trying not to become too much like one another. And yet the very suggestion that she might become "like me" sets up a sexual tension that culminates in union — "How Love burns through the Putting in the Seed."

Resist? It seems hard to imagine why either one would try. Although the result is birth — animal or vegetable — the act "is the sweetest dream that labor knows" and is justly marked by the medial capitalizations. Even though the poem resolves on the "watching" for the seedling to "shoulder" its way out of the earth, the true sense of completion rests on line ten. The everyday has been abandoned, the sexual tension has not been resisted, the act has been accomplished. The watching is mere afterthought to the real work of propagation.

And I say afterthought not lightly because once the seed is planted — in whatever sense you care to read that — the male work is done and he becomes unnecessary in a biological sense. It is only because we are human, and have agreed by tradition or habit or law to co-provide for offspring, that we share the "watching" and a sense of awe at the "sturdy seedling" that pushes forth. This coupling, as it were, seems more than hinted at by a very subtle prosodic move: the first part of the poem, I have called it a nine-line octave, ends with the first sentence (the five-line sestet is likewise one sentence), but the rhyme for the concluding line, "Slave to a springtime passion for the earth," appears in the second part of the poem, thus linking them in the slight but undeniable way we are linked to many things.

This sense of awe, of regeneration, is tinged with colorings Frost may have caught from Thoreau, specifically from "The Bean Field" chapter of *Walden*. But it is more attitude than image or language: "Ancient poetry and mythology suggest, at least, that husbandry was once a sacred art; but it is pursued with irreverent haste and heedlessness by us.... We have no festival, nor procession, nor ceremony ... by which the farmer expresses a sense of the sacredness of his calling, or is reminded of its sacred origin" (Thoreau 137). "Putting in the Seed," I think, seeks to return to ceremony, if only on a small scale, to take a cue from the farm and abandon oneself to the tug of sexual desire. If celebration is gone from the level of the community, the poem suggests, then let it remain with us two who are a community unto ourselves. Come to me in the fields after I have been gone from you all day, and let's see what sorts of attraction we can resist. And with that idea planted in her head, he goes off to the field to watch for her "arched body," shedding its encumbrances and restrictions, coming to him in the evening light.

The two parenthetical lines — five and six — are often remarked upon because of their awkwardness, but I think they are less awkward than they are an aside, a playful and sexually charged remark that introduces and establishes the growing sexual tone in the poem. Less could be made of these lines, perhaps, if they did not draw attention to themselves by differing from all of the other lines (and not just because they are parenthetical). Both lines are swollen to six stresses, and this lengthening helps to soften the lines. Heavy with accent, they are more sensuous, almost lush.

As Frost remarked, most people saw only his dark, harsh, masculine side. But there is a very secure, nurturing, feminine side to him as well, and I believe this is one of the poems that displays that side. Of course this is only one side in a complex mix of personae, and it is not my intention to suggest that this is even the dominant persona here. It merely complements the others, particularly the witty proposionist who seduces us into his sensuous world along with his wife. As I said at the outset of this discussion, this is a masterpiece, and it is a shame that it is an all-but-forgotten one.

"Range-Finding"

> Originally sent to Susan Hayes Ward, Christmas 1911, as "The Little Things of War." Published in *A Mountain Interval*, 1916, and reprinted in *Complete Poems of Robert Frost*, 1968.

William Pritchard has remarked about this poem that it is "strange, toneless." And I think that is right, but no more so than "Neither Out Far Nor In Deep" is strange and toneless in order to heighten the effect of the statement the poem makes. Pritchard also discusses the poem as one of those Frost kept back from his earlier books in order to have some strong ones on hand.

It is an odd war poem because there are only two military words in it — "battle" and "bullet" — and they are at opposite ends of the poem, so their effect is minimal or, perhaps more calculatingly, minimized. Even though there is more botany, ornithology and arachnid language here than military, this seems to me exactly a war poem, one that treats what the Gulf War strategists referred to as "collateral damages," the unintentional, and by extension civilian and puny, losses with respect and a quiet dignity. It is all observed and reported so matter-of-factly that it almost seems to be seen (emotionally) from a great distance, through a scope or a pair of binoculars. Yet the detail is so minute that we know the observer is, like the one in "The Vantage Point," very close to what he's observing.

A spider's web, a flower and a bird's nest are the victims here, though only the flower is injured, "cut" and "bent double." But even so, the butterfly returning to the flower is only momentarily put off by the fact that his resting place has been altered. The mother bird returns to her young, and the spider is merely disappointed that the bullet passing is not a fly. And yet, even these actions are too overtly stated and make it appear as if there is some consciousness at work here in this kingdom, a consciousness that could somehow comprehend the human forces at work and be saddened or sickened by them. There is not.

In other words, the great affairs of men have little to no lasting effect on nature. Rather than nature reacting to or reflecting the battle as a romantic would have, here the modern poet images nature's indifference with these tiny shrugs of the shoulders. In the natural world, Frost tells us, it does not matter at all how the damage happens — by bullet or hail, boot or wind. It merely happens as part of life, and no amount of sentimental anthropomorphizing on our part is going to make the least bit of difference. And that is the very troubling point here. If nature, and I mean by that all living things *not* human, is not affected by humanity, has no sympathies toward us one way or the other, then we are utterly alone. We have only ourselves to communicate with, and when communication fails, we have only ourselves to fight with, to kill. Look at us, he seems to prod, all alone in the void, only ourselves to care about our fate, and we go on killing one another as if anything mattered that much.

This is a poem that expresses grief, not a grievance — a distinction Frost makes very clear in his introduction to Robinson's *King Jasper*. This is a long-term and intense fear, a working out of some very deep suspicions about our kind in a poem that very clearly melts down to a wisdom made even more terrifying by being realized in miniature. The focus may be minute, but the theme is gigantic. He has found the range for us all, and it is limitless as we stand at its center.

The poem's circularity may at first be disconcerting. The sestet picks up and expands the opening line of the octave, going back to the previous evening when the web was strung in a remote and seemingly uninhabited "upland pasture." In almost magical terms, which are in direct tension with the flat tone, Frost describes the spider's web appearing like a "wheel" out of nowhere "o'ernight." By morning it is silvered with dew and thus visible. It is this tiny miracle and its life-and-death consequences that are set in contrast to the massive undertaking of a battle and its human life-and-death consequences. By immediately establishing setting—"The battle..."—it is rendered a backdrop, and whatever else happens is always in relief. Because "the battle" is backgrounded, the miniature action in the foreground is not consumed. To the contrary, the tiny foreground scene is in balance with the background, but presumably more important, human scene. The scenes are thus paired and balanced despite the disproportion in the size of the two actions. Just as Frost is fond of holding two opposing thoughts simultaneously, so is he fond of balancing ideas and problems, especially if the two are immensely mismatched in some way. By circling back to the opening image in the sestet, the backdrop having been established, he can get back to the small drama, suggested in line one, and watch it through. The spider, by line nine, has grown in stature because of the zoom effect of devoting all six lines of the sestet to him. As in "A Considerable Speck" we are forced to ask ourselves if anything living is too small to command our attention. And by our response, "no," the thing itself grows naturally by dint of our giving it our attention. Although this is a very homo- and egocentric reading of Frost's method here, it ironically provides us simultaneously with a way out of those eccentricities, namely by allowing us to focus on "the other."

Prosodically there is little to comment on here. The most remarkable feature may be the poem's regularity. It is 87 percent iambic (nine metrical substitutions), which also contributes to the flatness of tone. Only Frost, I think, could work his speech patterns along such a strict meter and not draw attention to his manner. He is wry and wily with his substitutions, and he is equally so when he is inconspicuously using regularity to another end. The most irregular line is, not surprisingly, the turn line, line nine. The opening pyrrhic followed by a spondee is effective in calling our attention to another scene and another time. The concluding iambic feet let us know we have not traveled far, though, and we are still on familiar ground.

This is a remarkable poem for the very fact that it avoids any show of pyrotechnics, either in form, language or prosody. It is quiet, and like the little things it recognizes as warranting recognition, it simply is.

Chapter 4

On a Tree ...

The Sonnet of *New Hampshire,* 1924

"On a Tree Fallen Across the Road"

> Published in *New Hampshire*, 1924, and reprinted in *Complete Poems of Robert Frost*, 1968.

For a 1942 anthology, *This Is My Best*, edited by Whit Burnett, Frost chose sixteen poems that had appeared in his books to that point. One of those poems was "On a Tree Fallen Across the Road." The critics, at least, would seem to disagree with this choice. Hardly a word has been written about the poem, and even Thompson fails to mention it. That is a shame, I think, because it is a good poem and deserves a broader audience.

I suspect the reason it was missed early on, even by reviewers, is that it is surrounded by poems destined for fame, the anthologies and the "Best" lists compiled by others. Consider some of the other poems that appeared in the volume: "A Star in a Stone-Boat," "The Ax-Helve," "Two Witches," "Fire and Ice," "Nothing Gold Can Stay," "Stopping by Woods on a Snowy Evening," "For Once, Then, Something," "To Earthward," "Two Look at Two," and "The Need of Being Versed in Country Things." And this is only a partial list of the best and best known of Frost's poems that appear in *New Hampshire*.

Poets rarely if ever are the best critics of their own work, and Frost, of course, is no exception. That he considered any of the sixteen poems among his best is interesting but not a reliable guide to what his best poems really are.

No two critics would compile the same list, so Frost's own choices are as suspect as anyone's, but this particular choice does make us pause and wonder why he thought the poem worth distinguishing.

"On a Tree..." is the only poem in the book with a subtitle ("To Hear Us Talk"), which, like the book itself, can either instruct or deliberately complicate our understanding of the poem. The subtitle remained ambiguous for me through multiple readings. First, there is only one voice heard in the poem, so the "Us" seems confusing, or deliberately misleading. However, the persistent use of "us" (five times), "we" (five times) and "our" (four times) finally insists that the "Us" is editorial, and the phrase takes on a whole range of possible meanings, not the least of which carries with it a self-deprecating "tsk

tsk," as if to imply how foolishly brazen we are to hold such attitudes in the face of the enormity of "Nature."

New Hampshire is filled with poems that exhibit mixed feelings toward nature and our place within it — or outside it. As many critics have accurately pointed out, Frost simply will not commit himself to a definition of or a position towards nature. If "The Need of Being Versed in Country Things" seems to express the belief that nature is indifferent, then "On a Tree Fallen Across the Road" expresses the opposite — that nature is consciously involved in our fate and only our resolve not to "steer straight off after something into space" keeps us from being defeated or at least bamboozled when the "tempest" "throws down" the gauntlet.

Although the poem says that we (humans) cannot be stopped from reaching our "goals" — whatever they are, "hidden in us to attain" — it stops short of giving us dominion over nature. After all, she can, and does, "halt us in our runner tracks" at will and causes no small amount of "debating" over what to do. The blustering tone is a serious *outside* Frost is putting on a tongue-in-cheek *inside*. In other words, the triumph he predicts has all of the uncertainty of any foresight and is dependent for any truth at all on the fact that we have, in our brief human history, managed to repeatedly survive whatever has been thrown at us — by us or by nature. It is, Frost would knowingly wink, slim evidence on which to prophesy a victorious future for humankind in what we insist on seeing as a battle between us and everything else.

It is, then, a poem of conflict in which little humanity tries to hold in balance big nature or big natural forces we are, realistically, incapable of fending off for very long. And yet with enough bluff and bluster and inflated ego we can convince ourselves a bit longer that the possibility exists — it could happen. The actual events of the poem are merely a cause for inconvenience. The incident is almost playful on the part of Nature (gendered female) as if life is a game. Even the tone of the poem is light and carries none of the darkly serious language or rhythms of some of the other sonnets. Yet here is where we must be most watchful of Robert Frost. Beneath the new snowfall, and that darned tree blocking the poet's way, is a whole sleighful of doubts about human's limitations and our ultimate extinction.

In addition to the shaky meaning of nature here, and elsewhere in the poems, is Frost's constant sleight of word — his seeming to say one thing firmly and absolutely but saying something very different, something vague and general and ungrounded. These questions arise from any close reading of the poem: what is "our journey's end"? What is "our way"? What is "the final goal"? Why is the ability to attain the goal "hidden in us"? And finally, what is that "something" we will not "steer straight off after"? These are puzzling in a poem that at first seems straightforward enough and, perhaps, a bit old fashioned in its attitude toward a nature that has sympathy or empathy toward us as a species. He hasn't, it might first appear, presented much of anything except a little tension between us and "it," "the other," whatever you care to call it, and a whole lot of questions that beg to be answered. But the only answers available are the ones we supply ourselves. Frost will not, as we have seen, provide answers that the reader must accept on faith. Rather, he prefers to remain in a Keatsian "negative capability," providing questions that become solely our problem if we answer them incorrectly.

Just what lies behind this prestidigitation in the sonnets is uncertain: is it playfulness? cageyness? caution? or a general unwillingness or inability to finally commit to any position that will make him answerable should he waiver? Unlike Whitman Frost seems unable or unwilling to say to us, to himself, "I contradict myself? Very well, I contradict myself," and unlike Pliny to say, "he ebbs and flows, his whole life a contradiction." Stability and consistency ultimately win out over the slightest possibility that he might have a change of heart.

For critics, of course, having a subject who remains constant in thought and practice over a very long career can be a plus because those ideas, beliefs, themes and habitual poetic moves can be watched as they mature and deepen but do not change, as such. There is something satisfying about finding statements and attitudes in *In The Clearing* that support and illuminate some made in *A Boy's Will*. In an unstable world there is something comforting about a statement of belief remaining true for over half a century — "They would not find me changed from him they knew / Only more sure of all I thought was true." But such consistency can, at times, seem more like stagnation, a reluctance to even dabble in a little change of attitude. This rock solidness, or rock headedness (depending on whom you talk to), is one aspect of Frost's attitude or position that his detractors often criticize. It is hard, in a poem such as the one under discussion, not to see their point, even if the aim is to celebrate the poems and their maker.

Despite all of our quarrels with his cantankerous steadiness, there is always one place we can look to and be again in awe, and that is in his prosody.

The only important metrical substitution from the iambic pentameter base in the first stanza occurs in the first foot of the second line. Here a spondee most aptly appears to emphasize the action, the challenge presented to humankind, which is represented by the sleigh driver and his companions. The tone, a deep bass, also suggests the first line of "The Lovely Shall Be Choosers," which appeared in the 1928 volume *West-Running Brook*, "'The Voice said, 'Hurl her down!'" Both suggest a higher power that ultimately has the power to destroy—despite the nonthreatening appearance of the act in "On a Tree...." The added emphasis of the spondee partially undermines such a reading and should establish in the back of the reader's mind, at least, that this tree didn't merely topple over. It was, in a sense, hurled down.

Another interesting touch appears in line five. Nature, through its actions, is interpreted by the poet as asking "who we think we are / Insisting always on our way so." Always one to exert his willfulness, especially within the poetic/sonnet tradition, Frost shortens the line to only nine syllables, as if to taunt nature, as if to say, I'll do it my way, thank you.

The trochee in the third foot of line seven has the curious effect of imitating a human foot crushing through the snow. It is a slight effect but nevertheless impressive, highlighting the poet's attention to minute details. The climb back up in "a foot of snow" is highlighted more than it would be in a regular line and helps to accent the word play between "runner" in line six and "foot" in line seven. Except for the spondee "Steer straight" at the beginning of line fourteen, there are no other major metrical substitutions in the poem.

It is one of the most regular of all the sonnets, Shakespearean, which may have caused it to be overlooked. Then again, it may be the quiet, completely conventional construction of the poem that suggested to Frost that this was among his best, since so few of the sonnets actually do "what they're supposed to do" as far as rhyme pattern.

4 : The Sonnet of *New Hampshire*, 1924

Although the poem represents a solid effort, and falls clearly into Jarrell's second third, why Frost chose it as one of his best remains a mystery.

The first two quatrains establish what is happening in the poem. The third quatrain and the couplet are syntactically joined to form a kind of sestet. Even when Frost goes conventional, as here with the rhyme scheme, he still can't pass up the opportunity to fool with the form internally, in this case by placing the turn in the Italian position, thus once more having it his way.

Line nine gives us a clue as to how to read the rest of the poem. The colon says that a list is beginning. "We will not," line ten begins, and then enjambs with line eleven. Because of the "We have" of line eleven we might be momentarily tricked into believing we have some structural parallelism here. We do not. There is parallelism, but it does not occur until line twelve, where Frost has mischievously left off the "we will" and thus created what can be confusion about what is actually being said (not an isolated occurrence of this practice). Once we realize that both lines ("though we have to seize earth by the pole / And, tired of aimless circling in one place,") are subordinate constructions, and the "not" is attached to "Steer straight off after something into space," we can possibly achieve a clear reading. Otherwise this is pure gibberish.

For all of its playfulness, all of its technical adroitness and all of its little-guy bluster in the face of nature, "On a Tree Fallen Across the Road" is, finally, a slight thing among the poems in general and not much more among the sonnets. Many poets would be proud to have a sonnet as good as this one among their own, and Frost obviously felt that way about it too, at least for a while in 1942. But given the many first-rate sonnets he wrote, this one just does not shine. That most critics have avoided this poem only deepens the mystery of why Frost was so attracted to it.

Chapter 5

Acquainted with the Night

The Sonnets of *West-Running Brook*, 1928

5 : The Sonnets of *West-Running Brook*, 1928

"Acceptance"

> Published in *West-Running Brook*, 1928, and reprinted in *Complete Poems of Robert Frost*, 1968.

In his essay "Robert Frost's New England," Perry Westbrook writes that "Acceptance," coupled with the much earlier "Trial by Existence," is an expression of Frost's puritanical "covenant-based theology" (242). And that, it seems to me, works very well for one reading of the poem. As we have come to expect, however, Frost's ambiguities rarely allow for one reading only, and this poem is a perfect example of how trusting a single reading can impoverish the poem and the reading process.

There are, to be sure, a number of places where alternative readings can occur or where, at the very least, there is some uncertainty of meaning. For example, the "something" in line six is a common hedge employed by Frost. But more on the mysterious bird number one later. Bird number two and Frost's interpretation of what he says (see the same ploy in "The Oven Bird") are the real problems here. More specifically still, it is the wording of the last sentence that leaves Westbrook's reading open to debate. If we indeed read the line to mean "let what will come (in the future) come," then his reading of the poem does appear to pair up reasonably with "The Trial by Existence." But "Let what will be, be" is not a simple, straightforward statement that all readers will interpret the same way. Consider these readings as well, both consistent with the syntax. "Let what exists, exist (or go on existing)," which is almost a plea to God, or whatever brings on and hence rules the darkness, to leave well enough alone. Or this: "Let (as in leave) what will exist alone" is perhaps a crying out against the darkness in defiance, a truculent little voice, so typical of Frost, against the immensity of what is and can't be changed.

It might be reasonable to suggest that the opening of the poem argues against such a reading—because Frost says nothing is "heard to cry aloud / At what has happened,"—but here too Frost has hedged by saying that "No voice is heard," which leaves, for me, a great open space in which much or many might be crying aloud out of earshot. In this reading, the subtext, again established by the spondees, is extremely important. It reads: "spent sun," "goes down," "burning," "too dark," and the concluding "be, be," the tiny voice proclaiming its existence to an indifferent universe à la Stephen Crane's "A Man Said to the Universe." Far-fetched, perhaps, but to a poet for whom "The play is all. Play is all," no possible reading can be overlooked or strongly discredited when there is a pattern to support it and a history of examples to be mustered.

"I was fooling myself along," he told Untermeyer about "The Road Not Taken," and one is entitled to believe that was hardly the only time. As we have seen so far, Frost is certainly not the "available" poet generations made him out to be. Better we should trust the poet who said, "I am not undesigning." And he is not, we might add, unsubtle, either.

What weaves through this poem is a complex of metrical structures, syntactic connections, and seemingly simple statements that are in fact implied contradictions, convolutions and ambiguities sufficient to cloud any clear understanding of what the poem says or what other poems it can be, or was intended to be, connected to.

I have already mentioned the subtext created by the spondees, a fairly typical strategy employed by Frost. But consider also the tension between knowledge and instinct represented by the two birds. Bird one, the female, seems to be a synecdoche for all "Birds" who "at least" know instinctively that it is only night coming on, and "murmuring something," she goes to sleep, presumably not caring much for what happens while she sleeps. However, bird number two, the male, "thinks" (a far cry from instinctive knowing) or "twitters" (says) "At most" a damnably complex notion in an equally complex statement after just having returned to his "remembered tree," where he has instinctively nested. Which is it, knowledge or instinct? Submission or defiance? Bird one or bird two?

Typically, we have no answer. What we do have are seemingly cooperating images that are really in collision. But Frost is so very deft at the placement of words that hedge a final commitment, that will not let "be be finale of seem" as Wallace Stevens wanted it. So perhaps the answer lies implied in the tension between "at least" and "At most." Or in an "as if" reading.

If a clue lies in the tension between "at least" and "At most," then bird number one is intimately connected to "The Oven Bird" because it is a "diminished thing," unable or unwilling to wonder at the change from light to dark or at the very least to utter a note of protest at the diurnal transformation of the world as she knows it. She closes a "faded" eye — here the adjective too suggests a diminished thing — and simply surrenders to what she cannot alter or even understand — or, in terms of "The Trial by Existence," remember. According to Frost's religious upbringing this would certainly represent an ideal situation, the weak individual accepting a fate that is preordained. However, I simply cannot read the title and see this as Subject Followed By Poem As Example. If that were so, that the title announces the subject and the poem provides the example(s), then where is the inner humor that must counterbalance the outer seriousness? Or vice versa (it is hard to tell which to take seriously and which to see as tongue-in-cheek).

According to this reading, then, "At most" must be seen as a foil to "at least," an alternative ideal in which the individual calls out against the darkness — the four occurrences of the word "be" — nearly a paraphrase of "Sir, I exist." (I am not, by any means, attempting to establish a Frost/Crane connection because Frost probably, at the very least, distrusted Crane's poetic instincts and practices, though I suspect some shared concern with an indifferent universe that could reply: "But that has not created in me a sense of obligation.") What I am attempting to establish is that there are two conflicted ideas at work here and that Frost seems to be drawn to both of them. Biographically, at least, most readers would associate Frost with bird number one, who would ideally surrender peacefully to a powerful God/force, but who questioned (sometimes more strongly than at other times) both in his life and in his art. Likewise, though genders are reversed here, the two birds seem almost symbolic of attitudes held by Robert and Elinor.

A more likely reading appears if we apply Frost's "as if" to the second half of the poem. The turn seems to occur in line eight, when the focus shifts to the male bird and the small, defiant voice calls out its existence. The minute seeking to call down, or at least hold at bay, the immense is in keeping with other Frost poems. Remember, for instance, the decimal point that separated the would-be lovers in "Meeting and Passing" or the blustering voice that proclaims eventual victory — "To hear us talk" — in "On a Tree Fallen Across the

Road" or the butterfly and spider surviving the attack in "Range-Finding." If only he could have it both ways, the poem suggests, to have in reality the ability to "be" both ways as easily as one can hold two opposing thoughts simultaneously.

But as I said earlier, the images of the two birds are in collision. They appear to coexist, but in fact they do not. They represent a crisis that occurs when desire is foiled by human limitations. We can see the ideas set metaphorically as two birds in front of us, but as two conflicted sides of a philosophy or religious construct, the problems become tangible and insurmountable. And that, I would contend, is what makes this more than a good poem. For here is Frost in the midst of "uncertainties, Mysteries, doubts, without any irritable reaching after fact and reason"— Keats' "negative capability." The real triumph here is that the poem melts to its final wisdom *because of,* not despite, "the uncertainties [and] ... doubts."

The bird's utterance in the last three-plus lines of the poem does not sound like resignation. Were the bird merely content to survive the night, then any tree would do. No, this "other," has plans, and those plans do not need to be hampered by knowledge of the future. To have the impetus to get on with life there must be uncertainty. If we know our fate, where is the incentive to do anything but wait for the end? Unlike the female bird, "Murmuring something quiet in her breast" and falling asleep, the male indicates little desire to do the same; in fact, he demands a darkness so profound it will obscure anything but what he thinks. Why demand darkness if one is planning to sleep anyway? No, this is a scheming bird, a dreaming bird, a bird suddenly safe and ready to plan a future, and to be left alone.

Like the speaker of "On a Tree Fallen Across the Road," who will not "Steer straight off after something into space," this bird is willing to stand hard by and face what is, without being encumbered by a future it can't control anyway. This bird may be Frost's idealized self, but it is surely one more admirable, one gutsier than the bird who falls asleep in the face of the unseen. Surrender is right in a perfect world perhaps but not in this one.

5 : The Sonnets of *West-Running Brook*, 1928

"Once by the Pacific"

Published in *West-Running Brook*, 1928, and reprinted in *Complete Poems of Robert Frost*, 1968.

From William Wordsworth's "The Prelude":

> *One summer evening (led by her) I found*
> *A little boat tied to a willow tree*
> *Within a rocky cave, its usual home.*
> *Straight I unloosed her chain, and stepping in*
> *Pushed from the shore....*
> . . . .
> *I dipped my oars into the silent lake,*
> *And, as I rose upon the stroke, my boat*
> *Went heaving through the water like a swan;*
> *When, from behind that craggy steep till then*
> *The horizon's bound, a huge peak, black and huge,*
> *As if with voluntary power instinct*
> *Upreared its head. I struck and struck again,*
> *And growing still in stature the grim shape*
> *Towered up between me and the stars, and still,*
> *For so it seemed, with purpose of its own*
> *And measured motion like a living thing,*
> *Strode after me....*
> . . . .
> *... but after I had seen*
> *That spectacle, for many days, my brain*
> *Worked with a dim and undetermined sense*
> *Of unknown modes of being; o'er my thoughts*
> *There hung a darkness....*
> . . . .
> *But huge and mighty forms, that do not live*
> *Like living men, moved slowly through the mind....*

The animated "craggy steep" that made such a strong impression on the young Wordsworth that he wrote movingly of it many years later in "The Prelude" is of the same stuff that became Frost's storm monster and is the source of untold numbers of nightmares. Precisely because we recognize this fear of nature, the nonsentient coming to life, looming up out of the darkness, that there is a familiarity that comforts in a bizarre way, a way that ties us with a bond of shared fear to every other one who has also been frightened. For that reason, I think, many readers are drawn to this poem and to the stolen boat episode in "The Prelude." And it is also, I suspect, what has attracted so much critical commentary and analysis to both poems.

I have no doubt that some variety of the story Frost told about the genesis of "Once by the Pacific" had a footing in reality, though which version is true we'll never know. But the poem itself is the product of a mature mind recollecting a boyhood fear. It is not the product of the fear itself, at least not directly. Many years of remembering and a shaping imagination have taken their toll, no doubt, on the original experience. Few of Frost's poems have been so investigated for their source, and none were subjected to so much mythologizing (by Frost himself). The poem is doubtless the best known and most widely commented on that we have looked at so far. And deservedly so. But speculation that the poem grew out of a fear of abandonment on the beach below The Cliff House in San Francisco in 1880 or a repulsion over seeing or imagining his parents together sexually (Holland 19–20) is a refusal to see this as a poem by a mature poet, not a confession from the psychiatrist's couch by a confused teenager. Frost was in his fifties when he wrote the poem. To suggest that he would have remembered across all those years such a complex of feelings attached to the experience requires a willing suspension of disbelief I am not prepared to make. Yet these are readings that have been put forth.

Instead, it seems more productive to confine our reading to what is known and what is discernible from the biography, the letters, the reported conversations and, most important, from the poem itself, which is, after all, the only reliable information we have. Lawrance Thompson's *Robert Frost: The Early Years* is a good source to look at for the stories.

The stories Frost told about the experience do not vary dramatically, and they all center on an unusually large and powerful storm that rolled in over the Pacific Ocean one night while Frost and his family

5 : The Sonnets of *West-Running Brook*, 1928

walked on the beach after a dinner at the Cliff House restaurant. Lagging behind mother, father and sister and playing with some seaweed, he apparently looked up and saw the storm approaching. His family was out of sight and he panicked, running down the beach until he caught up to them. The poem, of course, contains none of this information, and knowing it may be interesting to the curious but is worthless in reading the poem as a poem, that is, in giving it a close formalist reading. And as Pritchard has pointed out, the best approach, the most fruitful approach, when reading Frost is one that is hard and close.

If the world is not to end in fire or ice, then perhaps it will end in water claiming the land, the poem seems to suggest. Given Frost's anti-Darwinian bent, it seems odd that the poem is a depiction of the world devolving, a reversal of the way things have been, a Yeatsian image of apocalypse.

I say it is odd that Frost should prophesy a devolution of the planet because a devolution strongly suggests evolution, just as a design has been conventionally used to prove a designer. Frost questions, and leaves unanswered, that notion in "Design," and perhaps the same strategy is at work here, in which case what appears up close to be an orderly, though violent, self-destruction may appear from a greater distance mere chaos, self-consummation, the serpent eating its tail. But for a poet who thought so much of designs and patterns, and even cast the two poems in question here as sonnets ("the strictest form I have behaved in"), it seems unlikely that he would embrace an arbitrary and chaotic universe. For in Frost, as in few other modern poets, we find an obsession with form. Without it there is little we can do in the universe but wait out the inevitable — death and nothingness. But that is hardly the poet of "The Trial by Existence," where all is design and pattern, whether we remember or not.

So the argument comes full circle. Frost may not have wanted to scare off his Victorian readers who balked with him at accepting Darwinism, but it certainly seems, from this more distant remove, that he was at least toying with the idea, throwing it into shape to see what wisdom might melt out of the delight. There is, of course, no definitive statement here. There rarely is. But there is a dark seriousness that goes unbroken from title to final period, and that itself suggests that Frost must have been chuckling somewhere behind this serious facade because rarely does he let an opportunity go by to "play" with his readers. And I think the clue is right in front of us.

"*Put Out the Light*" is the clue. Whether one embraces creationism or evolution, the "light" is going to go out. Thus, by having a conclusion that does not commit to one theory or the other, Frost stands somewhere in the middle (of "uncertainties, Mysteries, doubts, without any irritable reaching after fact and reason"), just as he does at the end of "Design." But who is God speaking to in the last line? That he is speaking, and not putting the light out himself, means pretty conclusively that someone is left. And that someone appears in line twelve — though who it is is unknown to the reader and presumably unknown to Frost, since he isn't naming names — a hedge all too familiar to his readers and a logical move if one is going to claim the poem as prophesy on all manner of occasions.

As far as *how* the poem works, I think John Robert Doyle, Jr., has it right. He writes: "Almost exactly as a storm grows, 'Once by the Pacific' grows as one line follows another.... In between the beginning and the end, the storm and the poem grow to a climax" (171). If there is any question that Frost was fond of letting form imitate statement, we need look no further than "The Vantage Point" or "The Silken Tent" for examples as extreme as this one. But I want to return to Doyle. He discusses the meticulous care Frost took to build the poem, the blending of concrete detail and abstract statement:

> The nature and magnitude of the "something" is developed by suggesting the need for defense rather than direct presentation of the thing against which the defense must be made. In these six lines a growing, expanding, ascending order exists, just as a storm cloud grows, expands, ascends as it advances: the shore of defense is backed by cliff which turns into continent, the night of dark intent stretches out into an age. Thus at the end of twelve lines the evil is attacking a continent and an age. (173)

Doyle concludes his analysis with a brief discussion of the aptness of the crucially placed "prepared." Although Doyle does not say it, it seems implied, or should be implied, that the preparedness must be of a religious nature, certainly not physical, and more than likely not intellectual either. "The shore was lucky in being backed by cliff, / And cliff in being backed by continent," but what are *we* backed by? What will support us against this age of relentless smashing and breaking? Again, there is no answer, merely an admonition to be prepared. "There would be more than ocean water broken" and, I might add, more than land broken too. This is a storm of monumental spiritual proportions that Frost trivialized by applying its prophesy to the break up of the Untermeyer marriage in a letter. By rights it captures one of Frost's "obsessive themes," that of man's extinction. Because it is so portentous, Frost may have deliberately trivialized the poem to make it easier for him to deal with its ramifications.

Whatever his motives — perhaps they were as simple as trying to further advance his claims of second sight — the poem remains a key one for understanding what many readers knew and Lionel Trilling put into words: that Frost was a "terrifying poet." Like "Acceptance," this is a poem that faces the unknown. But unlike that other sonnet or "On a Tree Fallen Across the Road," this one cannot even muster the bravado to fake self-belief. The best we can get here is a storm warning. The attempt at a light closure, with "Before God's last *Put out the Light* was spoken," is a high-level, intellectualized whistling past the graveyard. What else is there to say in the face of what one believes to be a terrifying absolute? A little joke, a little shrug, a shuffle out of town. That is a gross exaggeration, of course, but the poem does lighten up at a key moment, one that is far more serious than a "lover's quarrel."

"The Flood"

> Published in *West-Running Brook*, 1928, and reprinted in *Complete Poems of Robert Frost*, 1968.

"The Flood" and "Acquainted with the Night" are back-to-back in *Complete Poems*. We read "The Flood" first, then turn the page and begin reading "Acquainted with the Night." We immediately forget about the former poem as we discover one of the truly great poems in American poetry. We also forgive Frost for the slight thing "The Flood" is. It is little wonder that both Thompson and Pritchard fail to even mention the poem. Although it may have been a small masterpiece for a lesser poet, it is not one we return to, even in a book that contains many more second- and third-rate poems than it does ones on the order of "Once by the Pacific" and "Acquainted with the Night."

Nevertheless, it is not without some interesting moves — prosodic and otherwise. But held up to "The Silken Tent," the truly great conceit sonnet, it becomes immediately obvious what the form can be and what it is not when it fails. This poem seems less successful because it does not arise out of an experience as do most of Frost's best poems. It is not dramatic, as he insisted poems must be. It seems forced and disobeys its master's rule that a poem "Like a piece of ice on a hot stove ... must ride on its own melting." And it sounds as if he had something to say, not as if he had a desire to discover something in the course of saying it.

In fact, "The Flood" disobeys nearly every definition Frost set forth in "The Figure a Poem Makes." I don't mean to come down with both feet on this poem, but compared to the great poems that appear in this volume, the shortcomings and the woodenness of the poem are blatant. Despite the title, the only real flood here is a few notable lines among the many that are paradoxically well contained. An argument could be mounted that a poem that deals with the uncontainable must be more strictly controlled than one that deals with what is already contained outside the poem, but no such argument would answer for the stasis all that control ultimately causes. No, this one merely reeks of the den and not the barnyard.

The doublings (and there are a number of them) in "The Flood" seem obvious, almost a matter of habit rather than a stumbled-upon opportunity. Internal rhymes double the rhymes of lines one and four: "harder," "water," "barrier," "slaughter." Then we have the sight rhyme of "choose" and "loose" of line five. A repetition of "blood" occurs in line six and of "brave" in line nine. Another repetition with only slight alteration in phrasing in lines nine and fourteen: "It will have outlet" and "Blood will out." The poem contains four sets of couplets, and there is a pairing of opposites in line ten: "weapons of war and implements of peace." A tour de force, perhaps, but to what end? What, in the poem's statement, is strengthened by these devices? It might almost be deduced that Frost is putting on a show, some sleight of hand, to distract us from the fact that beyond the showmanship the poem plods, stalls and seems more contrived than any other sonnet we have looked at so far.

"The Flood" is a conceit, and blood is the synecdoche for life, death, war, anger, rage and kinship that dominates the metaphor. The poem is a meditation, or a rumination, on the nature of humanity — a hot-blooded, illogical, uncontrollable nature — which the poet does not lament but merely, almost dispassionately, accepts as the way things are and the way things are supposed to be. In a way there is an acceptance, a resignation: "And now it is once more the tidal wave / That when it has swept by leaves summits stained." A sober fact. The heights of our history are marked by blood. The eras of peace are not so colorful, neither are they summits in most views of history. Whereas "Acceptance," "Once by the Pacific" and "Design" all question the nature of being, "The Flood" seems merely resigned to an inevitable "There shall be wars," and there is not even a hint of a shudder at the horror of that.

Perhaps that is what is most disconcerting about the poem, what makes it stand out from the others. The great poems of "negative capability" leave out any answers, present us with questions to ponder, leave faith hanging in the balance. "The Flood" does not. It offers an unshaking finality: "Blood will out. It cannot be contained." Not "will not," or "has not," but "cannot." This is not the fear or the terror that shapes many of Frost's best poems. There is long-range observation — that we will go on killing each other because we have always done that — and short-range observation — "We choose to say it is let loose by the devil," which is ambiguous and could be read as, "we choose to blame the devil, but we know it's really God" or "we choose to blame the devil, but we know it's us, our nature." But that ambiguity is not enough to give the poem the power or the horror of the two possibilities we are left with at the end of "Design" nor the stone-ground fear at the close of "Once by the Pacific" or the sheer human loneliness of "Acquainted with the Night."

In short, "The Flood" seems too pat, too easily satisfied with easy observations. Its own devices, the machinery of the poem, are showing. And perhaps the final blow, the conclusions of the poem seem more settled for than settled into. But as I said at the top of this discussion, Frost can be forgiven easily enough as we turn the page to "Acquainted with the Night."

"Acquainted with the Night"

> Published in *West-Running Brook*, 1928, and reprinted in *Complete Poems of Robert Frost*, 1968.

This sonnet has drawn more commentary and analysis than any other except, perhaps, "Design." It has been dissected, discussed and reassembled whole so many times that it seems superfluous to add another voice to the mix. So for this discussion I will paraphrase, quote and, I hope, synthesize the significant commentary that exists and address one or two items as necessary.

There is a very real temptation to simply quote the analysis of John Robert Doyle, Jr., and be done with it. It seems absolutely right, concise and thorough, and I will begin with it. He writes: "Much that is basic in Frost may be found in 'Acquainted with the Night.' While maintaining an illusion of artlessness, the author has not only used the difficult Italian terza rima but has made the form more difficult than need be by adding characteristics of the French set forms and of the sonnet" (166).

Doyle goes on to discuss the "rigid relationship between stanza and sentence pattern." He points out that "I have" sentences appear three times in stanza one, twice in stanza two, once in stanza three and no times in stanza four. Sentences that do not start with "I have" appear in the opposite order. He further points out that punctuation follows a similar pattern. "This mathematically progressive loosening of the sentence pattern is balanced by the fact that the formal pattern becomes most rigid at the very point at which the sentence pattern has become loosest" (167).

Although the phrase structure may appear simple, that is an illusion and adds to the ambiguity of the opening (and closing) line. How are we to understand "acquainted?" "Neither common usage nor scientific definition tells the reader what it is that the speaker knows when he says he has been acquainted with the night" (168).

5 : The Sonnets of *West-Running Brook*, 1928

The charge that Frost would not enter the woods or the darkness is often leveled against him. And it seems here, with the word "acquainted," that Frost is playing with that accusation, really flaunting it before the reader. The seriousness, the tone, the dark images are set firmly against the relatively lightweight "acquainted," a word that suggests not a deep and abiding relationship or knowledge of the night but a knowledge that is incomplete. This is a poem often pointed to to prove the "terrifying" underlying meaning of some of Frost's poems, but it seems more likely that this is yet another case of the poet "fooling himself along" and making much ado about relatively nothing. He is serious as hell on the outside but having a grand and giddy time on the inside. If this is Frost surrendering to the invitation/temptation of night, then it is a rare occurrence. Seamus Heaney says that "After Apple Picking" is the one place Frost surrenders to the woods (*Voices and Visions: Robert Frost*), but I am not convinced that this is a corresponding surrender to the dark.

Doyle next questions how we are to understand the use of "night." Is it physical and literal, or is it symbolic? He concludes that it is "ultimately symbolic" (169) and represents "the basic isolation of man from other men and from nature.... Perhaps the most significant aspect of the poem is that the fact of isolation, or aloneness, is never linked with complaint" (171). And as Frank Lentricchia points out in his *Robert Frost: Modern Poetics and the Landscape of Self,* "A deeply etched pattern of movement of the solitary man in Frost is being extended in [this] poem: we reach back to its origins in his first volume of poetry, in 'Into My Own'" (76). So there is continuity, even if the facts have moved the persona from projection (in "Into My Own") to fact (in "Acquainted with the Night").

But the literal night must also remain in mind, for Frost has presented some pretty harrowing nights in his poems — "An Old Man's Winter Night" and "Storm Fear" come immediately to mind — as well as spiritual nights — "Acceptance," "Once by the Pacific," "Bereft" and "Design," for example.

In Doyle's quite comprehensive analysis of the poem he also enters the fray concerning the "luminary clock," coming in on the side of those who contend it is really "unearthly," that is, the moon. Edward Stone, in his essay "Other 'Desert Places': Frost and Hawthorne," connects this poem with Hawthorne's "Night Sketches," which contains some common elements and situations—city clocks, lights and a watchman. For Hawthorne, Stone suggests, these are symbols of civilization and comfort; for Frost "'the luminary clock against the sky' ... peers through the darkness from the starlike distance of Crane's verse or Hardy's fiction...." (285). But it is ultimately a real clock.

Doyle's explanation of why the walker of the poem is out walking at night, because "He is walking for the walk," strikes me as an oversimplification. Even his added, "and for the chance to be alone, and for the chance to have contact with the 'night,'" does not seem sufficient reason. On one level this is clearly a dark night of the soul, and perhaps "not only a night, an age." If this is so, then a jaunt to the edge of town and beyond just to stretch his legs and commune with darkness and his thoughts is off the mark, despite Doyle's supporting quote from "Hyla Brook," "We love the things we love for what they are." No, in the face of the utter indifference depicted in the poem (climaxing in the line "Proclaimed the time was neither wrong nor right")—by time (in the first two tercets); space (in the fourth tercet and the couplet); people (in the third tercet) and nature (throughout)—something closer to an answer comes from "A Servant to Servants," when the speaker says, "the best way out is always through." Be it a crisis of faith, existential angst or the working out of a poem (Frost, according to Thompson, did much of his writing at night) or an idea, the only way to deal with it was to go out and back, that is to say through it, lest it control you, rather than you it. It is an essential pattern in many of Frost's poems.

Doyle concludes his discussion by saying, "One line of the poem indicates that 'night' represents the sadness that life has to offer, but much more important are the lines pointing to the fact that 'night' symbolizes the basic isolation of man from other men and from nature" (171).

And that, as I have previously indicated, I agree with completely.

Frank Lentricchia discusses the implications of homelessness in the poem, concluding, "The cruel irony of his 'acquaintance' with the night surfaces when the poem circles back to repeat its opening line which now begins to implicate the real state of the human condition with the state of darkness itself—they are reciprocally complementary" (77).

George Nitchie, in his notable *Human Values in the Poetry of*

5 : The Sonnets of *West-Running Brook*, 1928

Robert Frost, says the poem records a "teleological uncertainty." He points out that where the stress is placed in "I have been one acquainted with the night," whether on the "I" or on the "have" changes the reading of the line significantly. Stress "'I,'" he says, "then clearly nothing happened.... But if the accent is shifted to 'have,' then the caesura after the first rain [in the line 'I have walked out in rain — and back in rain'] takes on additional depth; something did happen, or at least may have happened.... We have no way of knowing.... Such a suspended conclusion may help to justify Louise Bogan's remark that 'Frost's later poems indicate that he knows more than he ever allows himself to say'"(39–40). In the same breath I should add that throughout the canon these kinds of ambiguities are common.

If the stress is placed on the "I" and nothing happens during those walks, then Richard Poirier seems justified in calling this a "terrifying poem about wandering off, losing the self, or belonging nowhere" (147). If it falls on "have," then the terror lightens, and there seems more cause to celebrate a discovery or some enlightenment, a positive something we are not made privy to.

Like Doyle, Elizabeth Isaacs has done a thorough analysis of the poem and has arrived at some different insights. For her the "'I' implies Everyman"(105). Ultimately this broader reading leads to this understanding: "...it strives to experience precisely the essence of man's existence in his lonely human state. As such, it becomes a universal elegy for mankind's aspirations as well as one man's personal lament" (106). Unlike Nitchie, who questions the placement of stress in the line, Isaacs says unequivocally that the opening foot of each line is a trochee, thus eliminating, for her, any sense of optimism. She further points to the present perfect tense as "suggest[ing] finality of the past" (106).

For Isaacs the city is all the more lonely for its inadequacy to comfort mankind in the face of loneliness. Lights, buildings, clocks — all of the vestiges of civilization — are unable to console him. The clock for her is no moon but "the final symbol of man's precarious efforts to measure and control the universe — 'to tell time' — to mark it right or wrong according to his own presumptuous mechanical standards. 'One luminary clock against the sky' shines in its little man-made brilliance, too high, too small, hanging against the vast darkness which he can never fathom" (107). This is an utterly bleak reading of the poem that does not even suggest possible alternative readings based on different scansions or interpretations of teasingly ambiguous lines such as "Proclaimed the time was neither wrong nor right."

Nor does Isaacs mention the playfulness (especially obvious among all this darkness) of the mirror-imaged "walked out" and "outwalked" of lines two and three. Yet it would be uncharacteristic of Frost not to include some kind of playfulness to undercut the darkest dark. Even the other great poems of human isolation — "The Most of It" and "Desert Places," with which "Acquainted with the Night" is often paired — allow a lightness in tone, image and language that Isaacs seems unwilling to see here. Hers is a solid, smart reading of the poem but one that seems to miss the subtlest subtleties, which ultimately suggest that perhaps it might not be that bad after all or at least not as suicidally dark as her reading suggests.

But Isaacs is not alone. Elaine Barry says quickly and finally that "Very few of Frost's poems are as unequivocally affirmative as 'Bereft' and 'Acquainted with the Night' are unequivocally negative" (102). Period, end of conversation.

William Pritchard calls the poem "extraordinarily undramatic, even mesmerized and mesmerizing in its sound" (189). And Thompson says, "RF was so constantly a Bible reader, and so familiar with so many famous Bible Passages, that the recurrence of the word 'acquainted' and the full title of this poem may be considered as echoing Isaiah 53:3: '…a man of sorrows, and acquainted with grief.'" (627). Note the hesitant "may be." It is prudent when reading Thompson to heed such markers.

And finally there is this from Randall Jarrell's outstanding essay "To the Laodiceans":

> What an already-prepared-for, already-familiar-seeming ring the lines have, the ring of that underlying style that great poets so often have in common beneath their own styles! I think that Dante would have read with nothing but admiration for its calm universal precision the wonderful "Acquainted with the Night," a poem in Dante's own form and with some of Dante's own qualities.... Is this a "classical" poem? If *it* isn't, what is? Yet doesn't the poem itself make the question seem ignominious, a question with a fatal lack of magnanimity, of true comprehension and concern? The things in themselves,

the poem itself, abide neither our questions nor our categories; they are free. (58–59)

I think little can, or need, be added.

"A Soldier"

> Published in West-Running Brook, 1928, and reprinted in Complete Poems of Robert Frost, 1968.

From the article in the title to the objective and distanced use of "body" and "spirit" at the end of the poem, "A Soldier" is impersonal, cold, an intellectual exercise that refuses us an identification with or sympathy for the subject. In line one, the soldier is transformed into his weapon and does not assume his actual "body" again until line thirteen. In between, "it," the "lance," becomes "they," "the missiles" in line eight. Why the switch to the plural is uncertain except, perhaps, that it underscores more boldly the existential "cringe" of line eleven — the limitations, again, of all soldiers.

But that doesn't seem sufficient reason to further complicate an already complex figure. Conceits are difficult by nature, but handled well, as in "The Silken Tent," they can be awe inspiring in their clarity and even their delicacy. "A Soldier" does not inspire, and in that sense it is closer to "The Flood" than to "The Silken Tent." It merely adds complications until the poem simply fails to hold up under the burdens. Try as I might, I simply cannot find the "inner humor," the touch of lightness that could very well salvage this poem for me. There are no chinks in this armor.

The three "lies" that appear in lines one, two and three start the poem out promisingly enough. It is an old Frost trick, to repeat a word or a form of the word in close proximity, and elsewhere it has proven effective in slicing through the "outer seriousness." It is a form of play. But here it demands only that we interpret, not that we enjoy the game. The lance that "lies unhurled" is a useless, impotent thing. That it "lies unlifted" shows it as helpless and perhaps hopeless as well. Finally, that it "lies pointed" in the direction it was heading, even though that direction appears arbitrary, yields the insight that "we" "like men" never look far enough—"neither out far nor in deep"?—and hence are denied a view of the enemy, who presumably stands at a greater distance.

These opening lines present several problems typical of Frost. It is only that here he seems either too subtle for his own good or so evasive, or vague, as to seem out of touch with his own meaning. He goes far afield to simply make one more figure of man's limitations. And what else, after all, is he saying in the octave? We fall short. And why are "we" "like men"? If we are not men, what are we? The only reading of the line that makes any clear sense is "like men"—in a tone that suggests "isn't it just like men"—yet that is not what appears. The figure is obviously a simile that compares the tenor "we" to the vehicle "men" in an attempt at clarification. Yet none is forthcoming from the trope, which merely serves to bring out the otherness of the speaker, who is only partly "like men," only like them in this limited comparison. If, however, this is a misreading brought about by overcompression of the language, then it is an avoidable problem, one that draws unnecessary attention to itself and necessary attention away from the poem.

The soldier is fallen, and our inability to ascertain his enemy is due to our shortsightedness. Or perhaps, as the sestet suggests, our sight is not so much short—"They cannot look out far"—as not short enough—"They cannot look in deep." This inability to know the self intimately is perhaps "the obstacle that checked / And tripped the body" and ironically "shot the spirit on" in spite of the lack of knowledge. As Frost closes "Neither Out Far Nor In Deep:"

> *They cannot look out far.*
> *They cannot look in deep.*
> *But when was that ever a bar*
> *To any watch they keep?*

Our inabilities may keep us limited and ignorant in life, but fortunately it does not prevent us from getting into heaven. As Jarrell remarked about "Neither Out Far Nor In Deep": "What we do know we don't care about; what we do care about we don't know" (43). But ultimately our limitations have ramifications only to us. "They fall" (missiles, lances, soldiers—they are all one eventually in this confusion of symbol, simile and synecdoche), but they only "rip the grass" and in the next line bounce their metal heads "on stone."

But perhaps there is the underlying humor, grossly and obviously unstated, that if we could stand back and view ourselves, scattering around, bumping into one another, falling down, being unable to get up and ultimately looking like a Keystone Kops short — in battle or in everyday life — we might not take ourselves so seriously. But we don't stand back, and the humor (if that's what this is) is darker for that reason. We have limited vision, and as Pogo has said, "We have found the enemy and he is us." We don't recognize our own irony. Our fall is exaggerated. "As fitted to the sphere" we are not yet ready to admit our own puniness. Yet finally it doesn't matter, not any of it, for whatever that "obstacle" is that shuffles off this mortal coil, it sends us off to a place brighter than we have ever seen or dreamed. This might answer for the vague and improbable use of "obstacle," which seems to downplay cause of death because life is precarious. In the end how we meet our end matters little, for the result is the same and we wind up back where we began — à la "The Trial By Existence" — preparing to choose the stuff of another life.

Because there is virtually nothing written previously about this poem — not even a mention in Thompson or Pritchard — it is pure speculation as to how intimately "A Soldier" is connected to any of the other poems discussed. But despite the lack of evidence or any reference points, the poem does not come close to the quality of these other poems, and it only gains importance by being compared to them and their clear expressions and "clarifications of life."

"The Investment"

> Published in *West-Running Brook*, 1928, and reprinted in *Completed Poems of Robert Frost*, 1968.

This is another poem that Frost's biographers fail to mention. And that is surprising because, as Richard Poirier says, it is a "sturdy little poem" (92). It is charming and "make[s] the best of what life has to offer" (Doyle 219). This is one of the poems that deserves to be read and appreciated, even if not worn out from many readings.

On a number of levels this is a curious poem. It is one of seven sonnets that offer the reader a question, or questions, but no answers. It uses two very unusual metrical feet in several places — the amphibrach (u / u) and the cretic (/ u /) — and the language is about as colloquial as Frost could ever hope to get. The humor in the poem comes as no surprise, but *how* he creates that humor is out of the ordinary. The poem "The Mountain" comes to mind when reading "The Investment," as does one specific line from that long, dramatic dialogue: "All the fun's in how you say a thing."

As Doyle points out, the three questions that form the sestet make it virtually impossible for the reader to determine which response to hold on to because each question demands a different response. Question one might elicit a "How wonderful" response. Question two might draw a dowdy "tsk tsk" or "Young people certainly know how to waste money." But the third question, the longest of the three, must surely grab our sympathies and our admiration for a couple who refuse to allow money to control their lives, even though that refusal may ultimately and ironically have made life more difficult. However, the "color and music" may very well counterbalance with spiritual benefits what has been impoverished economically or physically ("unearthed potatoes" that are "winter dinners"). But we do not know, finally, which question is the right one, which to respond to, so we cannot respond at all with any certainty (221).

Regardless of this problem, the poem presents an action against a life difficult with hardships and poverty. It does not bluster with statements about human superiority as in "On a Tree Fallen Across the Road," but is. The action is completed. Whichever circumstance is correct — good fortune, youth, or old age — it is a triumph over practicality, some whimsy in a bleak and worn out world. "The reader is inclined to feel good, inclined to feel that here is an example of human strength and courage great enough to meet the world's challenges" (Doyle 221).

The metrical substitutions in this sonnet run about double Frost's typical 20 percent. Such substitution is not unheard of, merely unusual. But the metrical feet employed are more interesting than the numbers. Spondees and pyrrhics are rare feet (I count five of each in this poem) but are fairly typical substitutions in Frost, as opposed to three-syllable feet. But curiously, three-syllable feet occur here in relative abundance, not the anapests and dactyls we find on occasion in other poems but amphibrachs (six) and a cretic, and all of them appear in terminal, hence rhyming, positions. It is as if Frost has dipped into some ancient metrical well (Greek, they have never been widely used in English) to underscore the curiousness of the poem's material and the "old, old house."

The amphibrachs appear in the first, fourth, fifth, eighth, tenth and eleventh lines ("Ŏvĕr|báck whĕre|they spéak|ŏf life|ăs stáyĭng"). The cretic ("Bŭt gét|sŏme cól|ŏr ănd|músĭc|oút ŏf lífe") concludes the poem. The feminine rhymes that result from the amphibrachs have the sense of sound trailing off and contribute to the strange double rhyme's effectiveness in each case: "staying/playing," "digger/vigor," "into/been to." The effect is a chilly but cozy scene observed through early darkness. The audible and visual are complementary but skewed from the expected. The painted house and the piano music seem out of place in a world cobbled together out of things that elsewhere pair, seeming as pathetically incongruous as a new car beside a falling down shack.

Granted, either the fourth or fifth foot of line one could be an amphibrach, but the double rhyme and the feminine ending — as mentioned above — throw most of our audial attention on the last foot. Although line one is enjambed, the parentheses in the second line cause the voice and eye to stop.

Simultaneously, the "as" and "staying" run together, fusing them into the amphibrach. Likewise, the cretic is a kind of culmination. The entire poem is about getting something pleasant "out of life." Hence, Frost has turned our expectations on us once again. He has already established the amphibrach pattern, so here, as a parting shot, he reverses himself, gathers his final statement and departs. One can imagine the surprise when the first amphibrach appeared, and the challenge and fun of working subsequent ones into a pattern.

A first response might be that these people have their priorities all mixed up. But then, who are we to say? In any of the three situations the questions suggest, the purchase of paint and piano are an extravagance but only because the house is "old, old," and is located "Over back." I don't know where that is and don't want to go there. Anywhere else these might seem reasonable investments, even necessities. But we must be careful not to impose snobbish practicality on poverty unless we are willing to impose it on wealth as well. The poem at least suggests that we should rejoice in this triumph over practicality rather than diminish it or make it appear foolish with an over-the-nose glare.

The amphibrachs and the cretic too are impractical, extravagant incongruities within the established iambic base of the sonnet. But so what? They work! They do not loudly call attention to themselves. They give a sense of rightness, of naturalness to the expression. How much would be lost to iambic insistence if the final line read: "But get some color and music *from* life"? A lot. The line is flat, toneless, awkward but metrically correct. But Frost did not write the line that way; he trusted his ear as the participants in the poem trusted their instincts.

The language of this poem is also quirky, playful and right. Rhyming the slang "ain't" with the formal "paint" (formal as in well-kept, not weather-beaten) is a risk that ultimately pays off. Just as the house is "renewed" by the paint, aren't we renewed by finding a poet using the ubiquitous "ain't" to make a cranky aside and make it sound exactly right? The "staying/playing" rhyme pits the static against the active, and the active wins out. As we later find out, this is vigorous playing as well as loud playing. There is an exuberance suggested that complements the wildness in the heart of the poem. Refinement may appear on the surface of these changes ("paint"), but underneath it is a rush to life. The listener who is "Standing still" and "counting winter dinners" may listen with only "half an ear," but whoever the piano player is is having one hell of a good time. Again, the active wins out over the static. The "turn" to questions in the sestet makes any answers irrelevant. Which question? All. And none. "Let what will be, be." Must we always have answers? The poem says no, sometimes just some "color and music" is enough.

The sonnets of *West-Running Brook* are a microcosm of the larger sonnet canon. There are the famous and the not-so-famous, the outstanding and the notwithstanding. We can divide these six poems perfectly along Jarrell's lines: "The Flood" and "A Soldier" should be torn out, though what they teach the reader about various of Frost's missteps should not be discarded; "Acceptance" and "The Investment" deserve our attention and respect; and "Once by the Pacific" and "Acquainted with the Night" are already acknowledged masterpieces too strong to be worn out and sturdy enough to withstand repeated deconstructions and reconstructions. This may be the slightest of Frost's collections to date, but at least for the sonnets it is the most representative.

Chapter 6

"The Master Speed"

The Sonnets of
A Further Range, 1936

"The Master Speed"

> First appeared in *The Yale Review*, December 1935. Published in *A Further Range*, 1936, and reprinted in *Complete Poems of Robert Frost*, 1968.

"The Master Speed" is an occasional poem — an epithalamium for Frost's daughter Irma and her husband John Cone. And given Frost's organic theory of composition, this fact makes the poem immediately suspect. The very concept of a poem written to order (even one's own order) negates a clear possibility of a poem beginning in "delight" and ending in "wisdom." It is at best difficult to imagine the implied objectivity of such a composition bearing up under the stress of a demand performance. Although the ideas and the metaphor of the poem are familiar (both are also central to *West-Running Brook*), familiarity does not predict a smooth melting of idea into poetry.

From the opening line there is a predictability to the poem. Even the form, elsewhere tested in numerous ways, is an exact Shakespearean form with only minor metrical substitution. The turn, intended, I suspect, to surprise, does not. It is merely perplexing. Given the "speed" and its accompanying "power," why would anyone choose to waste it standing still? If Frost had not been such a fan (and student) of contrariness and treated the theme of bucking the flow many times, his reluctance to embrace it here might not seem so odd. But he did admire the movement against the expected and accepted while simultaneously embracing the expected and the accepted. That tension invigorates more than one poem. Yet here the notion that "It is this backward motion toward the source, / Against the stream, that most we see ourselves in" (*West-Running Brook*) is reduced to "That you may have the power of standing still — / Off any still or moving thing you say." I say *reduced* because the couple is informed, perhaps advised, that they may choose to stand still, to not "climb / Back up" through space and time. Granted, the couple is not being told not to do these seemingly positive things. They are merely being told they have options, but why bring it up if there wasn't at least a suggestion that this was preferable?

"The tribute of the current to the source," which was celebrated in *West-running Brook*, is now conjured into stasis, the focus shifted from the formerly admirable contrary notion to nothingness achieved by husband and wife, a power they are endowed with on completing their marriage vows. Now, Frost is a great poet of marriage, but the strength gained here seems only that which allows the husband and wife to stand still rather than use their speed to run happily counter to the rush and flow of the rest of humanity. We must question if this is truly a gain for them. If it is simply power gained by uniting, by number, then this power to do nothing — as opposed to the alternatives suggested — seems hardly worth the effort. (This aspect of the poem is discussed further in the "Unharvested" analysis below.)

Many of Frost's most outstanding poems ask questions they never seek to answer. But "The Master Speed" raises questions that seem unanswerable. For example, it does not seem impertinent to ask who has bestowed the "speed" and "power" on the couple, or if it is theirs and theirs alone? Or, given the power that they have apparently had bestowed on them, and the tremendous possibilities it suggests, why would they choose, as previously asked, to spend it doing nothing? (As Frost wrote, "Strongly spent is the same as kept." Yet he appears to advocate the opposite here.) Why is it speed they are given with their union and not strength? None of the questions, it seems to me, are answerable within the context of the poem. And the reason for this is that the sonnet is contrived. It builds on an illusion that holds up only if it is not looked at too closely or logically.

So perhaps all of this is unfair to the poem. As Frost said to Louis Untermeyer, "The trouble with this sort of criticism is that it analyzes itself — and the poem — to death. It first depersonalizes the idea, then it dehumanizes the emotion, finally it destroys whatever poetry is left in the poem. It assumes that poetry is not only an art but also a science; it acts as though poetry was written in order to be dissected and that its chief value is its offering a field-day for ambiguity hunters" (quoted in Cook 352).

To accept such a quotation without reservation would of course deny that such analysis has significant value. Yet to reject it out of hand is to deny the magical, the mystical, the unnamable "freshness deep down things" that is at the very heart of poetry. Frost's remarks were made in regard to "Stopping by Woods on a Snowy Evening," a poem that had the depth, the inherent structural and poetic integrity to stand up to literally any amount of tempering and dismantling — and the poem has yet to lose its poetry.

But "The Master Speed" is another case altogether. It does not have the force of structure or idea or image to withstand close investigation. It is a fragile thing, a fanciful idea cast as a wedding gift for a daughter and son-in-law who would not seek to interpret it. And maybe that is the only spirit the poem can and must be considered in. As a literary performance, it is slight; as an idea, it is questionable; but as an ideal quantified into a poem it is all that it presumes to be. It is equal to the moment. It falls comfortably into Jarrell's second group of poems, the group that deserves to be read.

In the end the poem seems to satisfy another Frost poetical theory, even while it runs counter to the organic ideas. It is one of those poems that, as Frost once wrote to Untermeyer, "suggest formulae that won't formulate — that almost but don't quite formulate" upon close inspection. The relative weakness of "The Master Speed" under close scrutiny is magnified by the fact that it is followed, four poems later, by "Design," arguably the greatest of all the sonnets.

Unlike "The Flood" and "A Soldier," "The Master Speed" begs to be seen out of the corner of the eye and at a distance, not full-faced and with a stare. Aslant and distanced, this poem retains a certain magic.

"Design"

> The first known copy of the poem was sent to Susan Hayes Ward in a letter dated January 15, 1912. It was then titled "[A Study] In White." It was first published in *American Poetry 1922, A Miscellany* as "Design." Reprinted in *A Further Range*, 1936, and in *Complete Poems of Robert Frost*, 1968.

Like "Acquainted with the Night," "Design" has drawn an immense amount of commentary, from Randall Jarrell's enthusiastic appreciation in "To the Laodiceans," to George Montiero's "Robert Frost's Metaphysical Sonnet," a very useful line-by-line comparison to the original "In White," to Richard Poirier's extended discussion of the poem in *Robert Frost: The Work of Knowing*. As with

"Acquainted..." it seems unnecessary to add yet another voice to an already remarkably harmonious chorus. A look at the major responses to this poem seems to be the most instructive strategy.

Jarrell's is a brief but intense discussion that begins: "This is the Argument from Design with a vengeance..." and continues: "...this little albino catastrophe is too whitely catastrophic to be accidental, too impossibly unlikely ever to be coincidence: accident, chance, statistics, natural selection are helpless to account for such designed terror and heartbreak, such an awful symbolic perversion of the innocent being of the world" (46). Jarrell must be given credit for admiring this poem into the place of prominence it enjoys today.

Following a line-by-line, image-by-image reading and commentary, he goes on to say: "'What had that flower to do with being white, / The wayside blue and innocent heal-all?' expresses as well as anything ever has the arbitrariness of our guilt, the fact that Original Sin is only Original accident.... [T]he name 'heal-all' comes to sad, ironic, literal life: it healed all, [but] itself it could not heal" (48). After a nod to the poem's literary forefathers — including Emerson, Bryant, Melville and the Puritan preachers — Jarrell concludes by saying: "This poem, I think most people will admit, makes Pascal's 'eternal silence of those infinite spaces' seem the hush between the movements of a cantata" (49).

The opening of Richard Poirier's discussion also seeks the influences on "design." He, however, finds the major influence in William James' *Psychology*. After a long quotation from that source, he quotes both the early "In White" and the revised version, "Design." Unlike Montiero, Poirier does not do a line-by-line comparison/contrast. What he does do is examine the independence from source, the maturity and self-assurance displayed in the 1922 rewrite. He says that "'Design' is a rather playful poem, much closer to the charmingly confident willingness in James to allow for alternate or conflicting possibilities" (250). As we have seen, this penchant for holding conflicting thoughts in the mind simultaneously is a hallmark of some of Frost's finest poems.

Poirier's analysis next looks very closely at the language of the poem and most specifically at the word "appall," which he reads as 1) close to pale, 2) as in "impaled" (the spider holding the moth) and 3) pale as in fence slat. He concludes this reading with, "Thus, an extended and potentially self-canceling reading of the line would be 'What but design of darkness to ... design'" (251).

His analysis runs to over fifteen pages and is worthwhile to anyone wishing to see the poem from multiple critical standpoints that are extended and wide ranging.

Also taken up by Poirier are the subjects of why Frost "found" the poem to be a sonnet, even in its earliest form; where the poem is situated in *A Further Range*; the five poems that follow "Design," forming a smaller design within the design of the volume; why it is a "political" poem and "social commentary." This later discussion is especially helpful in understanding the advertising language and rhythms that appear in the octave. As summary, one paragraph deserves an extended quotation:

> It might seem as if Frost's attitude toward design is at odds with his earlier confidence in the virtues of form, but no contradiction emerges if it is kept in mind that from the beginning he demonstrated a habitual suspicion of any form or "design" or "provision" that does not find itself by almost lucky accident. Form, like the act of love, induces a sense of pleasure and security which fortunately cannot be permanent. If it were, the form would be without the efficacy and pleasure that comes from the act of discovery and shaping it, time after time. (258)

Although Frank Lentricchia's comments are very brief, they do serve to hold the poem differently to the light. He writes: "[T]he 'design of darkness' ... is first, and perhaps last, a metaphorical projection of the brooding, philosophical mind, not necessarily a reflection in poetry of ontological fact" (99). He goes on to support this: "Frost counterpoints a mechanical, nursery rhyme iambic rhythm against a scene of Natural horror. The effect of such counterpointing is two-fold: first, it heightens the macabre quality of the scene imaged; second, it implies the pressure of a self-conscious poetic craftsman.... [T]he poet's self-consciousness saves him; it allows the pressure of a difficult situation to be released" (99).

The sonnet may have been the "strictest form" Frost "behaved in," and he may have done so by "pretending it wasn't a sonnet." But if Lentricchia is correct, and there is no reason to doubt that he is, there is good reason to believe that Frost was probably extremely grateful for a poetic design historically fecund and readily available in those moments when doubt loomed large. I would not call it hubris, exactly, but control in the shape of "form" must have been very welcomed, a "momentary stay" of proportions beyond the sonnet's meager size.

Although most of the critics writing on this poem speak of the persona more as a philosopher, plumbing the depths and distances of man's thought, Elizabeth Isaacs sees the "scientist-poet" of the octave becoming the "philosopher-poet" in the sestet. First there is the observation of "weird combinations of existence" (115), the horrified wondering at how these elements, all grotesquely obvious in their whiteness, could come together at this moment, in this place before the "eye's microscope." It is, Isaacs asserts, "one of the best examples of Frost's existential poetry" (115).

After discussing the whiteness of the scene, and what the lack of color symbolizes in Frost — "snow, isolation and death" — she returns to the coincidence of these three coming together:

> The almost-but-not-quite possibility of this luminous trio, brought together out of the huge gloom of a dark universe and spot-lighted before the wary eye of the poet, magnifies the coincidence from microscopic to macroscopic terror in his mind.... If this incident can possibly have been planned and designed, then it is impossibly terrifying.... If it is unplanned, then life is utterly desolate in connotation; and thinking man must reject this idea if he will live with sanity and die with faith. (116)

The language of the questions in the sestet — "steered," "brought" and "thither to that height" — says Isaacs, all suggest a designer, a system controlled. And the direction in which we are steered by such language serves to intensify the "casual" "If" of the final line to the terrible size that it assumes.

Isaacs's is a solid, straightforward formalist reading of the poem. She is deadly accurate in pointing out the shift of language and focus that occurs simultaneously with the turn of the sonnet. Hers is a very useful discussion for any student of the poem or of Frost in general. Her apt analysis lays bare the very essence of Frost's poetry long missed by earlier critics.

Elaine Barry's discussion of "Design" in *Robert Frost* is valuable for its no-nonsense approach. But it breaks virtually no new ground. She makes it a point to note the double design of the poem — sonnet and "traditional sequence of logical debate" (89). She also points out

6 : The Sonnets of *A Further Range*, 1936

the irony of this too-white world finally being summed up in "design of darkness." Barry's brief comparison of "Design" to "In White" offers a nice introduction to the method of George Montiero's "Robert Frost's Metaphysical Sonnet." However, the latter essay is much more illuminating.

Prefacing his line-by-line comparison of the two versions of the poem (1912, 1922) Montiero writes:

> In paradigm, "Design" expresses those perplexing fears spawned and scattered by evidence which indicates that (1) human existence continues without supportive design and ultimate purpose, or (2) human existence is subject to a design of unmitigated natural evil. The details of the poem appear to sustain these complementary readings without choosing between them.... It is one of those rare poems achetypal to the entire ouvre of a poet, which in brief compass offers a valuable key to a poet's richness and reach. (333)

Montiero makes essentially ten major points about the differences between the two versions of the poem, concluding that the revisions show maturity, a constant faithfulness to the sonnet form and a deepening belief on Frost's part in the irony of both the argument and his poem.

The first point Montiero makes is that "Design" is more narrative than "In White," thus making the incident more mysterious and shifting the focus onto the spider. Secondly, he claims, and rightly so, that little of the original manuscript is left after the revision, and the changes make clear the genius of the poet and the poem.

Point number three concerns the shift in language in the revision toward more charged words — "dimpled," "fat," and "white" replace the more neutral "dented," for example. His fourth point addresses the omission of the "limp, lifeless" fourth line of "In White" and the improvement of the poem because of it. Points five and six are discussions of "kitchen domesticity" and the advertising language that is intertwined with it.

The change from "beady" to "snowdrop," and from "moth" to "dead wings" is Montiero's seventh point. Both changes, he points out, underscore the "childlike" description of line one. Point number eight echoes Jarrell's observation that the repetition of "heal-all" magnifies the irony that it can heal all, but it cannot heal itself.

"And of night," the end of line thirteen in "In White," is merely repetitive, Montiero observes. However, the resonant "to appall" in "Design" refortifies the power of bringing "design" and "darkness" together in such close proximity.

Montiero's final comments concern the closing line and the cumulative effect that "govern" offers because of its close relationship to "steered" and "brought." The comments are all insightful and instructive. The running commentary also serves to illuminate the achievement of each revision and the depth and enrichment each brought to the poem.

On the sonnetness of the poem he writes, "That the poem was conceived in the form of a sonnet, I would propose, is the poet's final irony, for the strict formal design which characterizes the sonnet apes and mimes the internal argument of the poem" (338).

That "Design" is almost universally admired needs only the quotations, summaries and paraphrases above for proof. I have not discovered any disparaging words or even any hints that "Design" is not first-class poetry. As Thompson points out, the poem was first published in the same year as Eliot's "The Waste Land." "Design" is as modern, as richly dark, as "The Waste Land." It is a poem not only representative of a good deal of Frost's work, but it also stands quite clearly as a beacon for an entire age and all of the doubt, fear, loneliness and uncertainty it reflected upon. As Borges has written:

"I think Frost is a finer poet than Eliot. I mean, a finer *poet*. But I suppose Eliot was a far more intelligent man; however, intelligence has little to do with poetry. Poetry springs from something deeper; it's beyond intelligence. It may not even be linked with wisdom. It's a thing of its own; it has a nature of its own. Undefinable" (qtd. in *Fighting Words*).

"On a Bird Singing in Its Sleep"

> Published in *A Further Range*, 1936, and reprinted in *Complete Poems of Robert Frost*, 1968.

Because Frost was so meticulous in arranging the poems within his books, it is impossible not to consider the connection between the poems that immediately follow one as strong as "Design" and how they may comment on each other or how they might address a common theme. Rarely does Frost follow a sonnet with a sonnet, but when he does (in *West-Running Brook* "Once by the Pacific" follows "Acceptance," and "Acquainted with the Night" follows "The Flood"; in *Steeple Bush* there are two sets of three sonnets) one of the pair inevitably pales in comparison. And so here "On a Bird Singing in Its Sleep" suffers by its placement as surely almost any other poem would.

This sonnet, written in couplets as are "Into My Own" and "The Oven Bird," is not as dark, as introspective or as questioning as "Design." The mood lightens considerably on leaving the former and entering this poem. In comparison, however, it is almost, in journalistic terms, a puff piece but only because of placement. Taken out of context it holds up well indeed. A belief in design seems inherent, both in the use of the sonnet and in the confidence of the persona in the less-than-dangerous actions of the bird. In the way the poem develops I am tempted to say that Frost's statement about "The Road Not Taken" ("I was fooling myself along") is just as applicable here. Just as that more famous poem contradicts every one of its seemingly concrete, absolute statements, "On a Bird…" even comes right out with the statement: "It ventured less in peril than appears." Indeed, lines three through seven make it very clear that the bird is not in any danger at all even though its song ends the moment after "the prick of hostile ears." But the other information given — that it sang only once a night, that it occupied no conspicuous position, that it threw its voice — should assure us via images what we may choose to reject in naked statement.

Frost is (no surprise here) having fun with us and our inherent fear of darkness and uncertainty masterfully examined in "Acquainted with the Night," "Once by the Pacific," and "Design" among the sonnets. Despite the overwhelming evidence that we have learned what actions are and which are not risky to our very survival and continuation as a species, there is always a nagging "what if," a tiny repressed fear lurking just downwind that we might, when we are most vulnerable, push too far (bird or man) and tip off our whereabouts to predators.

The persona of "The Road Not Taken" assures us in the closing line that "that has made all the difference" after repeatedly saying that all things being equal our road was the same as the other. Here we are assured that the bird has inherited enough tactics, that its half-song sung once a night and thrown ventriloquist-like out of an anonymous bush has not put it at risk. And yet the poem depends on our resistance to statement, to being told what to think, especially in the face of what we know, the vulnerability we've felt, the death we've seen even in the safest places. Gut reaction tells us the bird is in danger no matter how soothed we are supposed to be by reassuring words. Words fail in the shadow of images.

There is a wink, of course, behind the statement, "It ventured less in peril than appears." We hear ourselves react: "Yeah. Right. We know the histories of serendipity — 'the interstices of things ajar' — that brought us here. It is a history mingled with luck and extinctions." The question of a design or a designer is no more answered here than in the previous poem. The questions merely carry over from one poem to the next, silently, insistently.

The double form — couplet and sonnet, like the doubled form of "Design" — once again provides the irony and begs the question: do we, in the face of such uncertainty, provide form like a safe house, a "momentary stay against confusion"? Or do we discover form, any form, proving that some design exists? Can we know the answers to these questions? If Frost does, he's not telling. Oh, there are hints and clues that form — found or fashioned — is ultimately our salvation, that knowing in "singing not to sing" is itself a form, a design, a complex configuration of signs, symbols and tacit linguistic agreements that "arrest disorder," that focus, at least for the moment, on one thing and not any of the other of all possibilities. That's form. There is not only a shapely arrangement of letters into words, words into lines, lines into stanzas, etc., not only an engaging idea, but also a sense, a logic, a little fragment of order that we must be tempted to point to as proof of design — if it were not for the fact that the bird is only half awake, hence half asleep in a world we cannot comprehend, a bird's world, except by extension and a good deal of faith. (Unlike the previous bird sonnets — "The Oven Bird" and "Acceptance" — this one does not translate the talk.)

All of Frost's major themes are here: isolation, limitations, extinction. But they are made less immediate by the effects of the couplets and the metronomic insistence of the iambs. If it were not for a few initial trochees — lines three, five, ten — and some terminal spondees —

two, three, nine — the meter might further lull us from the uncertainty of statements of certainty and force us to believe that in repeated and repeatable regularity there must surely be the final assurance of design.

The three bird sonnets form an interesting triad. If the brash and tuneless oven bird was a diminished thing — within a diminished landscape — and the little he-bird of "Acceptance" murmurs "let what will be, be," then what are we to make of the bird singing in its sleep? Is it even more diminished? Has it finally found comfort and rest the other two had not? It is difficult to go beyond questions, for there are no certain answers, at least none that completely satisfy.

Frost clearly identifies with all of the birds. The reduced landscape of the oven bird is certainly, in part at least, the modernist waste land. The bird in "Acceptance" prays for "night ... too dark for me to see / Into the future." And that is not hard to understand given the future predicted in "Once by the Pacific." So has the bird of "On a Bird Singing in Its Sleep" become the patient "etherized upon the table" by the uncertainty and doubt in poems such as "Design," realizations such as the one in "Neither Out Far Nor In Deep," loneliness as in "Bereft," or the isolation in "The Most of It"?

As much as I would like to "Drink and be whole again beyond confusion," I think the map that connects these three poems — and many others in between — is not clear enough to provide surcease from confusion except to show in their author a sense of uncertainty that seemed to deepen even as his puritanism and conservatism heightened. Richard Poirier would make this a political poem, and we are certainly in the midst of Frost's politicalization in the thirties, but it rings truer, for me, as a poem that throws the bird of design into the light at a new and different angle, and finds it still uncertain of its wings. For design does govern in all three of these poems to one extent or another. Yet "On a Bird..." strikes me as the most chilling of the three. "The Oven Bird" can still look disapprovingly at diminishment, the bird of "Acceptance" seeks unconsciousness (on many levels), but the bird here has found it. And in its sleep we see mirrored the false confidence that closes this poem. Behind the absolute certainty of "It could not have come down to us so far" is a voice praying for assurance (note the aural pun on the poem's final word, "prey") that what he says is right. I think we can say with some certainty that not only is Frost humorous when he is most serious, he is also most uncertain when he is most cocky and absolute. After all, the only way to make the bear back down is to roar back in his face. What else is this little "inborn tune" than spit in the eye of forever?

"Unharvested"

> Published in *A Further Range*, 1936, and reprinted in *Complete Poems of Robert Frost*, 1968.

This, the most questionable of the poems I have listed as sonnets, was discussed at some length in the Introduction. That discussion revolved around the poem's sonnetness and how it serves as a companion piece to "The Oven Bird." There are, however, some other connections I would like to discuss.

Unlike "Design" and "On a Bird...," "Unharvested" seems to posit or accept a certain design without question. There seems to be, behind the scene presented, an intricate, known and frictionless system against which we can only occasionally hope for the extraordinary. The unexpected is so much celebrated here that the designed — the system, the controlled world (as safe as it would seem, as much as it would be welcomed) — in the two other sonnets is here powerful enough to want relief from. This background world, the "stated plan" and "routine road" are stifling, an overheated room, a regimented life suffocating under control and order. Walls and roads dominate. Their orderliness denies chaos with shape and direction, so much so that the random (though shapely) pattern of dropped fruit and foliage are a welcomed relief. We can only guess at the ecstasy of the scent of apples in a world otherwise devoid of scent. "The scent of ripeness" does not appear to override any other scent. It is suddenly there as if all else has been deprivation.

This celebration of randomness starkly contrasts with the previous sonnets, so the prayerfulness of the second stanza begs for "something"—twice! And likewise, it is one of the few places in the canon that Frost allows himself the extreme of an exclamation point. It is all as if to say: Enough. We need surprise. Regulation, design, and form are all well and good (the two previous sonnets are much more regular, as if clinging to form) but what we need is variation, a break, a risk. And the deep freedom taken with the sonnet form provides that variation, at least for the moment.

In a very literal sense "Unharvested" is also intimately connected to "The Master Speed," at least in a limited, but important, way. "Unharvested," by my reading, serves to clarify one mystifying element in "The Master Speed," that is, why anyone would choose to use this gift to stand still.

The connection between these two poems comes in a subtle, unspoken way. "But in the rush of everything to waste, / That you may have the power of standing still" the newly married couple are advised. In "Unharvested" that power becomes much more obvious. For, what is the "apple fall" but a "rush to waste"? And what is the "stall" but the "power to stand still" and enjoy the stolen scent? Once this sort of rare moment is imaged, rather than cast in abstract language, the "power to stand still" becomes very obviously a benefit to aesthetic appreciation rather than an impediment to climbing "Back up a stream of radiance to the sky, / And back through history up the stream of time." Placed against such power the scent of apples might be classified as mere minutia, but if the designed worlds that both of these poems strongly suggest are as rigid as they seem, then stolen moments, rich with scent or taste or texture out of the ordinary are rare enough for us to want to halt the ordinary powers to enjoy them.

Whether it is a life, a world, a universe designed to the extreme or a world devoid of anything but random, accidental and occasional form, it seems obvious why a poet would halt and celebrate what breaks from the habitual, happily discovering the sonnet in the experience as he goes.

Chapter 7

"The Silken Tent"

The Sonnets of *A Witness Tree*, 1942

"The Silken Tent"

> Originally published in the *Virginia Quarterly Review*, Winter 1939, as "A Praise for Your Poise," presented to Kathleen Morrison, Frost's longtime secretary and friend. Reprinted in *A Witness Tree* (which was likewise dedicated to Kathleen Morrison), 1942, and in the *Complete Poems of Robert Frost*, 1968.

"The Silken Tent," like "Design," "Acquainted with the Night" and a few other sonnets, is a masterpiece in the form, "probably the most poised sonnet of his career," says William Pritchard. And indeed none of the other thirty-six sonnets have the same feel as this one does. The single-sentence metaphysical conceit seems to drift from the top of the page to the bottom like a bolt of silk flung out. There is not a hitch or a pause. The logic and the poem unfurl seamlessly together. Perhaps only Petrarch and the seventeenth-century metaphysicals produced anything like this twentieth-century tour de force.

If most sonnets, as Frost said, stretch or compress to fulfill the fourteen-line requirement, then this is one of the rare exceptions that seems the ultimate wedding of material to form, form to logic, and logic to image.

Kay Morrison was a longtime friend of the Frosts. When Elinor died, Kay took over her secretarial and sometimes social duties. The poem was presented to Kay Morrison (Pritchard reports that the poem existed before Elinor's death, so the inspiration is not solely Morrison's) when it was first published in 1939. It is interesting, if of no critical value, that so soon after Elinor's death Frost was seeking new female inspiration. The reward, "The Silken Tent," as reported by Thompson, was a symbol of more than friendship and fondness. What inspires a poem, or a poem's revision, however, takes a distant second place to the fact that it gets written.

At first glance, the poem seems faultlessly Shakespearean, and the rhyme scheme supports that throughout. The turn does not occur in line thirteen, however, but in line nine, where Petrarchan sonnets conventionally turn. The images to that point have all stressed the freedom of the tent/woman, and the fact that there are grounding "guys" and a central pole are downplayed against the freedom of "swaying." Her soul, signified by the center pole, is likewise free and aimed at heaven. She certainly "Seems to owe naught to any single cord."

But the sestet (*efefgg*) focuses on the "bondage," the "countless silken ties of love and thought." Very gently the illusion of complete (or nearly complete) freedom is revealed to be just that, an illusion. The tent, and by extension the woman (the tenor of this extended metaphor), is indeed "bound / By countless silken ties of love and thought / To everything on earth." Both flesh and spirit are bound.

Suddenly, the apparent freedom and simplicity of the octave gives way to a complex of connections that suggest far-reaching ramifications and potential complications. In the octave the sibilants that abound [dis]guise (see the pun on "guys" in line four) the sensuality and sexuality in the images. In the sestet they tend to underscore the increasingly obvious images of bondage. It is certainly soft-core and harmless, but for blatant sexuality this poem has few peers in the Frost canon. Absolutely none of his poems that bristle with sexual tension come close to the perfect harmonization of all of this poem's parts and at all levels those parts are working on.

The poem displays utter restraint, and the seething sexual undertone is strengthened because of this restraint. It holds back, and holds back, letting the sibilants (like a woman walking in silk stockings) and a few well-placed words be all that he will admit. The rest of the tension comes from the denial and undercutting by actual statement of what is so obviously intended in image and sound.

I think it no accident that the language and the devices (alliteration, internal rhyme and pun) become more obvious in the sestet. If anything in the poem can be said to be tough, then the language sparingly toughens in the sestet: line nine contains both "strictly" and "bound"; line ten contains "ties"; line twelve has "taut." Line fourteen actually contains the word "bondage." Note here a second, almost self-mocking, pun in "slightly taut," suggesting a sexual naivete. But none of this suggests that "The Silken Tent" can support a full sadomasochistic reading. It cannot. But at the same time the underlying, and steadily affirming, sexuality cannot be denied. This is adult coaxing, teasing, flirting and complimenting of a very refined sort, a healthy, intelligent man's response to a healthy, intelligent, poised (albeit married) woman in the most sophisticated form human beings have yet devised, the love poem (and better still, a sonnet). If there is any reader of Frost left at this late date who still clings to the "homey" image of Frost, the New England poet, then let them read this sonnet closely and often. Those sibilants fairly dance with the images in an intricate and delicate, but hardly fragile, ballet. Only those in complete puritanical denial could miss the sparks.

And all of this is mustered by the deft handling of a single sentence that slows with judicious end stops and quickens with enjambment. There is but one caesura in the entire poem, a comma in line nine.

It must also be recognized that the sensuous images and the sibilance work directly against what is actually being said. Yes, the words "strictly," "bound," "ties," "taut," and "bondage" appear in the sestet, but each is either used with a negative or in a context that directly denies (or at least seeks to lessen) any sexual connotations. This does not mean that we should not recognize the power they exert in the accumulating sensuality, but their context has to be acknowledged. "Strictly held by none." "Loosely bound." "Silken ties." "Slightly taut." "Slightest bondage." Hardly the stuff of pornography or even a Harlequin Romance. But certainly this is a masterful blend of language, poetic devices and form that creates a tension absolutely palpable even while literally denying that it means that at all.

The two epigrammatic short poems that open *A Witness Tree* set forth the religious and secular concerns and design of the volume. There is at least a hint here that Frost could see where the secular and the parochial crossed, even if they did not merge. Although "to heavenward" and the mention of "soul" in the next line hardly constitute the poem's focus, they do add a level of meaning. That these words appear at almost the exact center of the poem invests them with symbolic meaning as well — in a roundabout way "heaven" and "soul" may be connected to death, which in the seventeenth century (where this sonnet has its firmest roots and closest relatives) was connected to orgasm, "the little death." In a poem rife with connections and allusions, it should come as no surprise if this were just another one.

Like any masterpiece, the poem seems bottomless and maybe a little elusive. Frost is not as forthcoming with affirmations of definitive readings as we might wish. Like the bright thing in the bottom of the well in "For Once, Then, Something" if you hold your head just right, squint ever so slightly, you just might, in the right second of an unannounced hour and day, catch it and say you're absolutely certain you think you have it right.

"Never Again Would Birds' Song Be the Same"

>Dedicated to Kathleen Morrison. Published in *A Witness Tree*, 1942, and reprinted in *Complete Poems of Robert Frost*, 1968.

Like "The Silken Tent" that appears eight poems before it, "Never Again Would Birds' Song Be the Same" is so quiet as to seem almost a whisper. There is a sense of relief that accompanies early readings of this poem mainly because it follows "The Most of It," one of the darkest treatments of human isolation to be found anywhere in Frost. Even to hear Frost read the poem (he does on PBS's *Voices and Visions* videotape) there is a sweetness, a lilting absolute lyricism that is too delicately balanced and certain of itself to be fragile. Also like the previous sonnet, it is masterful and perhaps even deceiving, for rarely is anything completely what it seems in these poems.

The poem develops by quatrains (even though it is stichtic in form), and the first two, forming a kind of octave, are knitted together by a single sentence that exists in both quatrains. Quatrain one establishes the influence of Eve's voice upon the songs of birds. Quatrain two says that a "tone of meaning" is also there, a slight addition to the first contention, but still an addition.

Lines nine through twelve could be considered the beginning of a sestet, with the more insistent "she was in their song" signaling a turn. Or it might be considered yet another addition to the building already in progress: she influenced their song; she provided meaning; she was too long an influence to be lost. If this reading is accurate, then the couplet turns on the idea that it wasn't merely happenstance that this occurred. It was part of the plan from the beginning, hence an answer seemingly out of "Design."

Two possible readings arise from this uncertainty. If there is an octave and a sestet, then the last line of the octave suggests a purely accidental influence on the birds. "When call or laughter carried it aloft," would indeed contradict the very direct final statement of the couplet, "And to do that to birds was why she came." The "that" of the closing line becomes suspect: what is "that," a purely accidental, undesigned influence on birdsong, or a deliberate, designed influence, an elaborate plan orchestrated by a designer to forever have the guardianship of humanity, proclaimed by God, be stamped even on the voice of birds, "a thing so small"?

I don't believe there is a correct way to read these lines. Both make sense. Both can be supported from a prosodic and conceptual point of view. And both readings are possible thanks to other problems introduced into the poem from the beginning.

Part of Frost's theory was that poems lead to "clarification[s] of life." But seven of the thirty-seven sonnets ask questions that never get answered, and many more (such as this one) raise questions that cannot be answered because Frost provided mixed clues, if any. Clarification, then, means that we are thinking clearly, seeing all points of view simultaneously and asking the right questions to keep all of this in focus. This does not mean we ask questions that lead to definitive answers. We simply ask questions that allow us to keep from being disillusioned by our unknowing. This is a tough equation, but we can accept ambiguities because life is ambiguous, and poems are about life. They show us a new way of seeing what we already knew.

For a poem that appears so quietly certain of itself and straightforward in its presentation, this is a mighty convoluted piece of work. But wait!

Two questions come immediately to mind, and these in themselves raise questions that are not, and cannot be, answered given what we have to go by. Question one: Who is "He"? There seem to me three possible answers, any of which can and do skew the reading of the poem. These readings are complementary but mutually exclusive.

Given the reference to Eve, the first possible speaker is Adam. If the speaker is Adam, then he appears to be saying that men are capable of good, of being a positive influence on the world (nature). The historical prospective argues somewhat against this identification of the speaker — it has "persisted in the woods so long." Yet still, who would know better?

God, perhaps? If God is the speaker (and He has spoken elsewhere in Frost), then we read a positive influence by Eve on the birds. But this, of course, must be counterbalanced, and this counterbalance occurs in the pun on Eve (darkness), which takes Adam's reading and stresses that along with the positive, evil was also picked up (however innocently) from the serpent. In this case there is a suggestion that the now-voiceless serpent has insured an evil influence by first going through Eve, thence to the birds through her. A circuitous route, to be sure, but one not denied by the poem. This reading is encouraged, in fact, by the very general "Her tone of meaning." Nowhere are we told if this tone is good or evil, if we are to read this with joy or with the resigned voice of one who sees the evil in the world and knows it cannot be stopped because evil will always find a way.

Not Adam? Not God? Who then? The third possibility seems to me to be the poet himself. Perhaps this is an appreciation of birds' songs, or natural beauty, a celebration of the creative influence of man on nature. In the "tone of meaning" then we have another restatement of Frost's poetic theory of the "sound of sense": "Her tone of meaning but without the words." After all, "The Oven Bird" offers much the same line: "The question that he frames in all but words." In other words, he has done it before, why not here, now? No reason. In the post-Edenic world we need to seek for something of our own making to praise, this reading suggests.

Which voice? Which speaker? The sonnet is sufficiently open to allow for any of these choices and sufficiently closed to omit the possibility of some sort of randomness as occurs in "Design." This is not coincidence, nor is it a random speaker. With randomness comes a whole new set of questions (Where does "He" come by his knowledge? is the first and foremost) that absolutely cannot be answered. The poem stumbles and self-destructs in the face of such a possibility. There may be another possible speaker, but it is not a random one or one designated an Everyman.

"Never Again Would Birds' Song Be the Same" is connected to other sonnets in several ways. The form is one way. The Shakespearean format, whether one sees Frost sticking to it or not, seems less important, however, than some other connections.

The poem is clearly connected to "The Oven Bird" by way of the "sound of sense." It is also connected because of the Eden/Eve references.

In this way it is also connected to "Unharvested." Although there is no pattern or dominant image (other than the references to the biblical fall), the power of each of these poems to summon the others is strong.

Likewise, "Never Again..." powerfully recalls the three previous bird sonnets — "The Oven Bird," "Acceptance" and "On a Bird Singing in Its Sleep." This is not a fourth bird sonnet per se, but it does call into question the certainty with which some statements are made. All three of the bird sonnets teeter uncertainly on the question of safety, the future, the present, for all of them depict frail creatures in a harsh world. This momentary, self-assured step into a fanciful world, gently but forcefully influenced by a woman's voice, is a far cry from the real world, where survival reigns and niceties of modulated "tones of meaning" hold no sway. Taken as an irregular but logical next poem, "Never Again..." seems to lean toward the harsher readings suggested above and away from the gentler readings that would force it to depend too heavily on the other three without, perhaps, the resources and strengths to stand alone.

In many ways it is easy to see why critics have read this poem as a fairly straightforward appreciation by Robert Frost of Kay Morrison after her years of service as secretary. It is a poem that is "the quietest and most discreet of his sonnets" (Pritchard 237), a poem that possesses "delicacy and firmness" (Pritchard 237), yet without some very deliberate digging it does not yield up a great complex of meanings. Perhaps, as with "The Silken Tent," we want these to be sonnets of wisdom as well, an aging poet's earned clarity, a poet "made whole again beyond confusion," a poet who, for the rest of us, can recognize that "Truth is Beauty," and say it elegantly, unambiguously and freshly. And perhaps that is just what he is doing — but I don't think so.

"Time Out"

> According to Lawrance Thompson, the poem's original title was "On the Ascent," and it was written in 1939. It first appeared in the *Virginia Quarterly Review,* Spring 1942. Reprinted in *A Witness Tree,* 1942, and in *Complete Poems of Robert Frost,* 1968.

With many of Frost's sonnets (as with the other poems) what is being said (subject matter) is as interesting as how it is said, and sometimes more so. "The object in writing poetry is to make all poems sound as different as possible from each other, and the resources for that of vowels, consonants, punctuation, syntax, words, sentences, meter are not enough. We need the help of content — meaning subject matter. That is the greatest help toward variety" ("The Figure a Poem Makes").

Sometimes how it is said provides a clue as to the attitude Frost took toward the poem. Certainly here form and subject are inextricably bound into a single statement — something like: we need to relax, to "pause" in order to realize not only our surroundings but the similarities and differences in things.

The poem is foremost a meditation on such matters and a demonstration of them at the same time. That Frost wrote the poem and the introductory essay to his collected poems — "The Figure a Poem Makes" — in the same year strikes me as significant. Each is there as demonstration and clarification of the other. The poem talks about the need to "pause" and reconsider the "context" in which we find ourselves. Simultaneously, the poem is relaxed — many lines have only four stresses (seven, eight, ten, eleven, twelve, thirteen), others have three stresses with one secondary stress (two, nine, fourteen), and one line clearly has only three stresses (six): "He followingly fingered as he read." In a sense this poem challenges the notion of what a sonnet is as boldly as "Unharvested" or any of the other highly irregular sonnets. But as it challenges our notions about sonnets, it reinforces the sonnetness of the poem by sticking doggedly to the Shakespearean rhyme scheme and turn.

The relaxed attitude of the reader's/thinker's head is held up to the straightforward stare of enemies (this image choice, no doubt, reflects Frost's awareness of the European war in progress). The "obstinately gentle air" is paired off against the harsh "clamor" of "cause and sect." These dyads are then mirrored by the relaxed meter and strict rhyme scheme. Both have their place, the poem shows us, because they complement each other. In this sense it is a charmingly unambitious lyric that gains additional respect for its unwillingness to screech or stamp a political foot to make the world sit up and listen. It wisely demonstrates the knowledge that when the shouts and other forms of patriotic noise die down, this quiet, assured little poem will still be

7 : The Sonnets of *A Witness Tree*, 1942

speaking for an audience that wants to listen, even long after the moment of its impetus passes.

Although "Time Out" contemplates war as only one of several images, it surely outdoes "A Soldier" and stands firmly beside "Range-Finding." Frost is always best when he approaches war obliquely, as those earlier poems attest and as will later ones in *Steeple Bush*).

The notion of a mountain being a "text" is a very contemporary one indeed. In an age that puts forth examinations of all manner of things as texts, can find nothing that is not a text, Frost, at least the Frost of this poem, would feel much at home but much dismayed at the extent to which this idea has been applied. The notion may have been whimsical on his part, but I suspect not. Birds' songs have been interpreted, the little dumb show in white has been witnessed and analyzed, the thrust of a parasol has been heeded, all in a sequence of sonnets — "The Oven Bird," "Design," and "Meeting and Passing." And all of these have been "oversounds," what is said "in all but words," ample demonstrations of his early and unstintingly adhered-to theories of the "sound of sense."

When Frost claimed that there was literary criticism in the poems themselves, I strongly believe he was referring to examples of his own "sound of sense," instances such as these in "Time Out" that are "done in plant," in other words "in all but words." He provided the contexts he mentions in "The Figure a Poem Makes" over and over again. Throughout the poetry we find, without even the benefit of a guide "Who only has at heart your getting lost," proof that the theory is true, and more important, that poems can prove the theory without our ever having to notice.

The original title seems to praise the human ability to think through, to rationalize, to separate the valuable from the valueless. It is very nearly a celebration of ideas out of the Enlightenment. Very nearly, but not altogether. It combines instead the pleasure of thought with the rugged pleasure of action, the pauses that action provide wherein we can contemplate and appreciate not only our own complex abilities with the brain but our complex abilities with the body. Regardless of the complexities of the other sonnets in this book, "Time Out" is as it appears, and that quality carries with it a sense of assurance that even simple observations are valuable as we scavenge the world and cobble together a life.

Chapter 8

"Etherealizing"

The Sonnets of *Steeple Bush*, 1947

8 : The Sonnets of *Steeple Bush*, 1947

The seven sonnets of *Steeple Bush*, which all appear in the "Editorials" section, show some major changes in the lyrical voice of Robert Frost. Accused of not being "modern" during the 30s because he didn't address the immediate problems of contemporary man in modern society, he seems here to want to atone for that misplaced accusation by completely reinventing his subject matter. Although his ideas remain intact, their presentation, by and large, is diminished. (Compare the opening of "Etherealizing" to these lines in "The Black Cottage" in *North of Boston* [1914]: "...why abandon a belief / Merely because it ceases to be true. / Cling to it long enough, and not a doubt / It will turn true again, for so it goes.") The power to startle the reader into a realization has become in many of the poems merely posturing and cleverness. If a poem may not be "worried into being," how then do we explain lines and whole poems that read as if they were tortured into existence compared to the graceful and natural-sounding earlier lyrics?

It's not that there aren't other weak sonnets (and other weak poems) in Frost's canon (remember Jarrell suggested throwing out a full third), but before there was always a solid poem to balance out the weaker ones. In *Steeple Bush* only "Directive" clearly presents the old Frost with all of his old power. Sadly, however, one poem is not enough to carry the entire collection. This is not the book to discover Robert Frost in, and it is, likewise, not the book for dismissing him either. To read, specifically, these seven sonnets is to make us that much more thankful for the enduring sonnets, the brilliant variations, the timeless contribution not only to the history of the sonnet but to lyric poetry in general.

"Etherealizing"

> Published in *Steeple Bush*, 1947, and reprinted in *Complete Poems of Robert Frost*, 1968.

Science fiction and some Puritan desire to scourge the flesh right down to the spirit seem locked in combat here. On one hand we are to visualize man reduced to gruesome gray matter spread along the beach with nothing left to do but dream (poems, presumably). Therein lies the sci-fi part of the equation. The spiritualizing part comes in the closing couplet, which, like the closure of "Unharvested," is very much a prayer or at the very least a wish expressed in the tones of prayer. And yet it comes to naught but cleverness. The old twinkle in the eye was once "the mischief in [him]" but now is merely a twinkle of self-contented gamesmanship — and no longer "for mortal stakes." Once "All the fun's in how you say a thing" had to be tempered with a goodly shake of salt; here it seems to be literally true. The wife of "Home Burial" says, "you think the talk is all," and here it has become its very reason for being, substance gone.

If this were all of Frost that existed, then critics who accused him of being too obvious, too clear (in modernist terms), would have been right. Except for the unexpected nod at evolution, an idea he had shied away from or subtly avoided in the past, the quirky reversing of the rhyme scheme from *abab* to *baba*, and the unexpected apocalyptic image of the brain sans skull and body, there is not much here lurking on the metaphorical playground. This is straightforward, and multiple readings are not rewarded with insight or realization of oh-so subtle phrasing. What you see is what you get.

But what does lurk about is a nagging question. Did Frost know that the poem was not only about the immaterial but was itself immaterial? Is that the joke here?

In some sense this is an aggravating poem to read. With all of the other fine examples of sonnets surfacing in the mind, there is almost a desperation to create some irony, to see some subtle feint, to discover a pun that will somehow validate the poem. But unless it is so very heavily protected by a code we do not know, I think it is merely what it appears to be. To the foursome "enough ... slough ... stuff ... rough," we might add "fluff" — not mockingly, but sadly.

"Why Wait for Science"

> Published in *Steeple Bush*, 1947, and reprinted in *Complete Poems of Robert Frost*, 1968.

If the previous poem projects a human race that has evolved

beyond the body to pure brain — or perhaps mind — then this one projects a need to devolve in order to survive an inevitable destruction of the planet. This is not a new image for Frost. Human extinction is an old theme for him and in the sonnets goes back to "Once by the Pacific," but here there is a twist. "Once by the Pacific" foresaw destruction as much natural as human-made — perhaps more so. Here humanity is solely responsible for creating "Sarcastic Science," which, with the two recent atomic blasts, had insulted millions of people to death.

This much more interesting poem does indeed feel as if it melted into existence. There is not the forced, arch tone of "Etherealizing." This is not to say that it ranks with "Design," "The Silken Tent" or the half-dozen other outstanding sonnets, but it does deserve a reading. As Pritchard writes: "...to complain that Frost's late poems are inferior to the others is to indulge in the complacency one has identified in the poems. Instead, they should be put in their place, which is a small one, and seen as relatively weak manifestations of what on other fronts still revealed itself— never more so — as a quite unbelievable energy of performance" (244).

It is tempting to read this poem as Frost's own growing recognition of his fading powers. In one equation (another sci-fi construction) Poet=Planet. The question becomes, as the poet/planet begins to self-destruct, how do you escape yourself? Your decay? An answer is, of course, only partly hinted at but suggests that a) because we were created, then we must be uncreated, or b) because we have evolved, then we must devolve. In either case birth, growth and maturation must be counterbalanced by death and decay. Organic. Simple. But typically we get only an "if" that echoes loudly the "if" at the end of "Design" and a shrug of the shoulders in the last line that reveals nothing but the persona's unwillingness to commit beyond that "if," that possibility. "Hardly" does not shut the door on his "amateur" answer. It simply renders it more tantalizing, the silence in its wake more bloated. This is certainly more reminiscent of the old Frost than most of the other sonnets here.

The temptation to construct an answer based on what is given here, to say we must die just as we always have, is to miss the wryness, the little wrinkle that "if" and "hardly" create, which will not let us finally say anything for certain. Even the sonnet's construction, the regular Petrarchan octave, is commented on by the irregular three couplets of the sestet. "Don't be too certain that you have it figured out," it seems to taunt; "appearances are only that — sometimes."

"Any Size We Please"

> Published in *Steeple Bush*, 1947, and reprinted in *Complete Poems of Robert Frost*, 1968.

I come closer to calling this a good sonnet than any of the other six in *Steeple Bush*. It has all the markings of a solid Frost performance: subtlety, puns, the gesture outward and the return to self. This is the third of a group of three sonnets. It is the first time he has grouped three sonnets together in a volume (he does it again one poem later), so we must presume there is a purpose.

"Etherealizing" predicts a strange evolution, "Why Wait for Science" an equally odd devolution. In "Any Size We Please" the persona seems to accept where he is, seems content not to reach heaven with his "infinite appeal," in fact, gives up by simply saying "'Hell,'" and remaining quite firmly planted between the two (the image apes Whitman's speaker in "Out of the Cradle Endlessly Rocking," anchoring earth and ocean).

This sonnet, like its triad-mates, shows signs that Frost recognizes his own failing poetic powers. But this poem takes a different tack. If the "he" of the poem is looked at as Frost only minimally disguising himself, then the dramatic action and the otherwise odd references begin to make more sense. The post–Elinor Robert Frost was biographically a "lonely case," and he feared much of his life for his sanity. The "half-mad outpost sentinel" begins to take on new proportions as self-reference because, among the moderns who mostly shunned him, he was an outpost sentinel guarding a tradition he felt was slipping away in a rush to find "new ways to be new." The dramatic spell, I suggest, is a thinly veiled reference to *A Masque of Reason* (1945) and *A Masque of Mercy* (1947), the latter published the same year as *Steeple Bush*. The "not without some shame of face" may be explained by this excerpt from Thompson: "Last night I finished writing the *Forty-Third Chapter of Job, A Masque of Reason,*" Frost had told a friend [George F. Whicher] in April 1943, in announcing completion of the first of two plays. "You may have to listen to it sometime when I have done its companion piece *The Whole Bible, A Masque of Mercy.* Neither may ever see the light. I will dabble in drama" (117). Thompson goes on to tell us that Frost "impulsively" spoke with a leading Broadway director before the second poem/play was complete, and he regretted it, chiding himself for his newest ambition.

The second quatrain of the octave contains a dramatic gesture ("a poem is only as good as it is dramatic") that seems almost typically Frost. He reaches up, like the "long two-pointed ladder" in "After Apple-Picking," "toward Heaven" in "infinite appeal." When there is no reply, he says, simply "Hell," creating and making clear at once the upper and lower boundaries of his universe (see line fourteen and note the pun "uni-verse," his unified poetry — "unchanged from him they knew") and his position squarely between them, complete with limitations and loneliness à la "The Most of It" and "Two Look at Two."

The reference to "science" in line eleven keeps the poem neatly tied to the previous two and takes what little energy is in those poems into itself and, not coincidentally, gives back to those sonnets considerably more than they had before.

"He had been too all out, too much extended" refers, in this reading of the poem only, to the drain on his energies the writing of the *Masques* had been. But then in a fine Frostian closure, again dramatic and humorous, he checks his wallet and the money thirty odd years of uni-verse had brought him in the "trial by market" and seems if not content spiritually then intellectually at ease (though certainly far from forthright with that kind of statement, it is only subtly suggested). He is still self-contained, self-reliant. "No one was looking," smacks of self-pity, but it very adequately sets up the self-embracing action of the closure, which seems to recognize how far he has really come (four Pulitzer Prizes and nearly universal appreciation). If the powers are failing, as these poems seem to recognize and rather obliquely examine, then there is a kind of acceptance in the couplet. It may be only a blustering gesture (one we've seen before), but it *is* a gesture — not stasis, not denial, but another manifestation of what Pritchard calls "a quite unbelievable energy of performance."

This reading of the poem presumes a Frost operating in the microuniverse of self, that all the references are autobiographical. An alternate reading to this one poses a macrouniverse, a place in which all of the drama is played out to an audience of none. It is a man gesturing, posturing, making faces at himself in the bathroom mirror. In this reading the self diminishes to a helpless, hopeless seed of itself and is dwarfed by the universe, not expanded as by a long, successful career of uni-verse.

Let the *Masques* be finally gestures to the heavens. I much prefer the man reflecting on his life, himself, large in the world of his making, a craftsman in a workshop he has every right to be proud of. This is the playful Frost so nearly lost in the other poems in this collection.

"The Planners"

> Published in *Steeple Bush*, 1947, and reprinted in *Complete Poems of Robert Frost*, 1968.

The tone and attitude of "The Planners" owe much to "Etherealizing" and "Why Wait for Science" and nothing to "Any Size We Please." The poem is clipped, breezy, intent on human extinction, but its serious intentions are forced to do battle with rhyming triplets whose insistent sound, accompanied by relentless iambs (until the last five lines) argue against seriousness and underscore the merely facile word and thought.

The opening triplet depends solely on the triple rhyme to succeed because the statement itself seems too obvious to need stating. Ditto the second triplet. What follows is interesting for only the shallowest of reasons. The pronouns require that our attention not wander. The rush of "thoses," "anyones," "thems," "theys," "theirs" and "theses" is dizzying and requires considerable disentangling to figure out who says what and who thinks what. This is painfully distant from the graceful syntactic unraveling of "The Silken Tent." The rewards for this chore are scant, and the most reasonable response to the whole endeavor is to say "So what?" The attitude is mock-political more than social or historical. The rap against socialism in the face of human extinction seems both nonsensical and puny.

The turn occurs in line ten with the first of two questions. So too begins the use of amphibrachs (u / u) to end the lines. Hence, all five lines of the closure have feminine endings. The triplet contains double rhymes "planners/banners/manners" and the couplet a shrug-of-the-shoulders smugness that is recognizable from the past but here seems impotent. Nothing is gained. Nothing is proven. Nothing is strengthened by this gesture. Where amphibrachs appear elsewhere ("The Investment"), they lend an air of quirkiness. They underscore the oddity of the poem's situation, but here they smack of showing off, like performing a few perfunctory technical backflips in an otherwise drab performance. How well, we are reminded, a few small moves can enhance a poem, and how just as easily they can look absurd.

"No Holy Wars for Them"

> Published in *Steeple Bush*, 1947, and reprinted in *Complete Poems of Robert Frost*, 1968.

Frost believed that poems should, for subject matter, concern themselves with what is known to the reader. Here, however, he seems hell-bent on overworking the obvious instead. That powerful nations take the spoils of war and small, weak nations get nothing seems too apparent to need saying and at the same time is myopic. The losers in World War II were ultimately winners in that untold dollars were paid out to rebuild what the powerful had destroyed.

The little exercise in "being" and "doing" that is played out in the first quatrain is not enough to save this poem from its own cleverness. If this is an "Editorial," what is at issue? Is there another point of view that might be argued?

It seems useless to belabor the point much further. Pritchard writes:

> When for a time it looked as if America, Britain, and Russia were the three powers in the post-war world, Frost wrote a sonnet …

mocking the little states.... In the poem's sestet he turned to God for his word on the whole matter.... Amusing enough perhaps, but complacent as well: herein speaks the Big Voice of the hugely successful poet who has seen them come and go. If the career which began in felicity were to end in publicity and in poems like "No Holy Wars for Them," maybe — the reader feels — it had better really end there. (244)

The fact that this is one of the few strict Shakespearean sonnets Frost wrote and that he has once again mustered the amphibrach (lines six, eight, ten, twelve — the d and f rhymes), but to no notable end, seems superfluous. In the end the poem seems just mean-spirited, a side of Frost more than hinted at (and more than likely inflated) by Thompson. What may have seemed to Frost more play (or worse yet patriotism) comes across as downright orneriness.

"Bursting Rapture"

> Published in *Steeple Bush*, 1947, and reprinted in *Complete Poems of Robert Frost*, 1968.

Akin in attitude to the previous sonnet — this is the middle poem in a second sonnet triad — it is likewise flippant, distantly cool and aloof. The two possible readings of the title — Bursting the Rapture or The Rapture Bursting may be symptomatic of this posture.

The poem tells us that farming (taming nature) used to be easy, but now science makes it harder. The only way to make a living is to get "science on the brain" (as in, perhaps, water on the brain?), and the poet is too old to hold up under this burden of the new world. The octave establishes the stress the persona feels in the voice of an aged farmer. The poem resolves with a sestet spoken by the doctor (the twentieth century's primary symbol of science), who consoles the patient by claiming that many have the same complaint. His banal prognosis is that pressure will continue to mount until it bursts like a brain aneurysm in the form of "a certain bomb" (please don't miss the play on A bomb here).

The use of "ecstasy" and "exquisite" to describe the mounting tension between nations, and the explosion of the bomb reduced to a mere headache, seem arch and too soberly awful to be said. What is lacking here is a sense of caring for the individual lives that were dispatched so dispassionately in an attempt at blithe humor — "Drop a nuclear bomb and call me in the morning," the doctor's tone suggests. It is distasteful and sad that the poet who wrote "Bereft" could resort to such repugnant social commentary. The "shame of face" he claims he felt in "Any Size We Please" is misplaced. It belongs here.

"The Broken Drought"

> Published in *Steeple Bush*, 1947, and reprinted in *Complete Poems of Robert Frost*, 1968.

Between the second sonnet triad and the final sonnet, "The Broken Drought," Frost placed two nonsonnets, a quatrain called "U.S. 1946 Kings X," which further gloats on the bomb, and "The Ingenuities of Debt," which offers us a crumbled city, failed ingenuity, in other words, extinction.

The final sonnet continues the theme of human extinction we suspected had been thoroughly trounced in the first triad of sonnets and in the previous poem. Evolution. Devolution. Science. And now nature is projected as the evildoer.

The octave is external, containing actions of various sorts: a stopped speech, rain, cheering. The sestet turns inward. It builds from reinforcing Frost's doomsday belief to hyperbolic questions about man's being on earth at all. He might well have turned to his own "Trial by Existence" and spared us his puzzlement. Line fourteen, then, questions God (again). It examines a psychological state wherein the speaker is so flustered that his theory about the cause and severity of the drought becomes more important than Christian thinking and tradition. For everyone else the drought is broken, but for the "prophet of disaster" it becomes another kind of drought — one of the spirit.

This poem seems to question, or at least to examine, the human ability to hope. The poem pits prophet against reality and shows us the prophet actually hoping to be correct just for the sake of being right and saving face. Compared to "Bursting Rapture," whose speaker ignores the multitudes who die, this poem is even more solipsistic, the speaker even more callous than in the previous poem. Here the entire earth is at stake and, as we saw in "Why Wait for Science," has no place else to go.

Another reading suggests that this is an editorial proclaiming the end of "The Waste Land." The prophet is T. S. Eliot, and he refuses to concede that the long war, begun in 1914 and only now over, heralds the end of Modernist Angst, that there was never any reason to imagine a "desert" world resulting from industrialism and spiritual diminishment. It is a jab or a poke or a slap, but it clearly — in this light at least — gathers together key images of the period and, in what we can only presume, proceeds to make his contemporaries hold to their visions and convictions in the face of his incontrovertible proof.

Either way it is a look at solipsism, though whose we cannot say. Frost's own darkness, his own modernist angst, is certainly still in evidence in *Steeple Bush*, but he too sometimes missed his own irony.

It is true that the sonnets of *Steeple Bush* do not rank in Jarrell's top one-third, and only one belongs in the middle third. They are, however, consistent, no matter how disturbing we find that consistency. The themes remain from the earliest poems. Frost is, as he predicted in "Into My Own" "[not] changed from him they knew." True, the powers that shaped the earlier poems are only hinted at here. The impulse to play in places and to chide in others is an echo of the past, but the mounting pressures brought on by his alter ego, the public Frost, may be as much at fault here as anything else. And having said that, I would find it hard to justify my last statement with any real conviction. The callousness, the jaded attitude toward mass death, is unpardonable and goes far beyond the urge to entertain. But clearly a number of forces were at work. The very existence of "Directive" among these other poems (and Thompson gives no hint that Frost had kept the poem in reserve for a long time) is proof that his powers could still be summoned.

Thompson tells us that Frost was certain that these poems were as fine as any he had ever made. The themes are in place; the technique is mostly still solid. But something fails in the spirit of the poems, and these *are,* ultimately, poems of spiritual concern. In the bravado, in the tough talk and the tough posture, there has been a change, from the belief in poems as a mighty offering to heaven, to an attitude that seems more like a spit in the eye of death, fame and posterity. What, one presumes, was meant to look feisty looks merely foolish.

Chapter 9

"Despair"

Other Sonnets

"Despair"

> According to both Thompson and Pritchard this poem was written at Derry — perhaps as early as 1900–01. It was sent with other poems to Susan Hayes Ward at Christmas 1911. The poem was first published in volume one of Thompson's biography, *Robert Frost: The Early Years*, 1966, and reprinted in *Frost: Collected Poems, Prose and Plays*, 1995.

William Pritchard has written convincingly about why Frost did not include this poem in the manuscript of *A Boy's Will*. As he aptly points out, nothing happens in the poem, and "its tone is monotonous, portentous, humorless throughout." He goes on to say that Frost was too close to his own dark mood to write well about it. He concludes: "'Despair' found no place in *A Boy's Will* therefore because its expression was 'forced,' its protagonist too passively in the grip of circumstances from the contemplation of which no 'poetical enjoyment' [Matthew Arnold's phrase] could be derived. And poetical enjoyment was the quality Frost sought above all others, whether in life or in literature" (15). Indeed, part of that enjoyment was in the composition process itself. "The poem should come as naturally as leaves to a tree, and if they don't they should not come at all," wrote Keats. Frost appears to have agreed completely, for he restated this organic idea several different ways.

A close look at the poem reveals none of the characteristics of good Frost sonnets. There is no sense that he is "fooling himself along" or that he is saying "one thing in terms of another." Even the "all" that figures so prominently in "The Most of It" is reduced here to a single meaning, which certainly contributes to the flatness of tone and the lack of energy the poem displays.

If Thompson is right, Frost was suffering a crushing depression as 1900 approached 1901. If the poem was written at that time it may well be that he was too close to the mood that gave rise to the poem, which would easily account for its woodenness. For a poet who stated that a poem "begins in delight and ends in wisdom," and further, "like a piece of ice on a hot stove the poem must ride on its own melting" (which is very nearly Keats), this is certainly a good example of what can go wrong when the poem doesn't come of its own accord but is dragged into being and shunted to conclusion by an impatient poet. Frost concludes "The Constant Symbol" by claiming "A poem may be worked over once it is in being, but it may not be worried into being.... It can never lose its sense of a meaning that once unfolded by surprise as it went." Wisely he left this one unpublished.

Among the poems Frost sent to Susan Hayes Ward in 1911 was "Despair." Previously he had sent her another sonnet, "Design" (then titled "In White"). "In White" was a weak poem that showed some of the same flat tendencies as "Despair." "In White" was, years later, brilliantly revised into "Design." But the same hand was never set to "Despair." Perhaps Frost recognized that the poem was beyond repair. But the fact that he could recite it from memory sixty years later argues against such supposition. I think it safe to suggest that the mood, the depression that was the impetus for the poem, was just too painful, and he chose to leave it be, perhaps as a reminder that poems can't be "worried into being."

The total self-absorption displayed in the number and positioning of first person pronouns is, I think, telling. Only three other sonnets—"Design," "A Dream Pang" and "Bursting Rapture"—begin with "I," and none of them use it with such insistence. "I" appears five times in the poem, "me" twice, and "my" twice. As the poem progresses it discusses the "dead diver" in such a way as to leave little doubt that Frost has thoroughly identified with him, so the third person pronouns likewise refer to the persona, thus adding four more self references. That is a considerable number and only goes to underscore the fact that Frost was not involved in "play" as we have come to expect, but is playing "for mortal stakes"—a very different game.

A glance at the poem's prosody reveals one line that may or may not have been consciously expanded. Line four is twelve syllables long, six metrical feet (there are no three-syllable feet to be found), and this may be a conscious or subconscious demonstration of his unwillingness to let go. That is small evidence to pin such a reading on, so I will not belabor the point. But it is interesting (given the habits Frost was developing at this time) to speculate that even in a time of terrific stress and self-doubt, there was still the urge to create, extratextually, a text not immediately available to the eye.

Except for some strategically placed trochees and spondees, there is little, prosodically, to distinguish the poem. The spondees again create a subtext — "dead diver," "held fast," "weeds' snare," "God let" and "warm light" — but not one at odds with the text, not one that creates tension or adds energy or interest. In the rhyme scheme we may be witnessing the genesis of Frost's penchant for combining sonnet formats, or creating variants, but he certainly has not hit the successful stride of 1906–07.

"When the Speed Comes"

> Written at Derry during the sonnet period about his experience in the Arlington Mill, 1893–94. First published in Thompson's *Robert Frost: The Early Years.*, 1966, and reprinted in *Frost: Collected Poems, Prose and Plays*, 1995.

If nothing happens in the sonnet "Despair," as Pritchard suggests, then perhaps "When the Speed Comes" is too busy, relentlessly compressing experience and ideas until Frost must in places rely on esoteric mill references and language that renders meaning difficult at best, impossible at worst. For example, "The music of the iron is a law" is so vague as to be meaningless, I suspect, to most readers. What is "the iron"? Is it that device for pressing cloths, or is it something else formally or informally called "the iron"? What is its function, and why is it law? Even in the context of the poem we do not, and cannot, know. This is not sloppy craftsmanship but a problem arising out of a clash between subject and form; that is, there is simply too much subject to fit in the form. It is not a simple matter of there being too much bread for the butter or butter for the bread; no, there is a whole meal that wants to climb aboard, and it just can't crowd on.

Thompson tells us that at the time Frost was working in the mill "he had admired the deftness of the girls who worked in the wool-dusty atmosphere, the quick motions of their fingers as they reached in among taut threads to snatch up broken ends and twist them quickly together. Now he began to feel that these girls were forced to become human spiders; that all those threads seemed to be drawn … from their insides" (*Early Years* 158).

If in fact that image was Frost's, then we have to marvel at the fact that he let it get away and settled instead for what we have in the poem — ambiguous, if not downright obscure, lines, and images that nowhere approach the interesting ones reported by Thompson. Whether it was Frost's failure to recognize the potential of his image of the girls, or Thompson improving upon or wholly imagining what the young Rob Frost *must* have thought, we'll never know for certain. But considering the number and quality of sonnets that came out of the same time period, I think we are justified in suspecting Thompson of engineering the reported images.

If we ask the same question about this poem as we did about "Despair" — Why didn't Frost include it in the manuscript of *A Boy's Will?* — I think the answer has more to do with the setting of the poem than it does with quality. Still, it is not of the same quality as the other poems in that book, or any of Frost's others, for that matter. In *A Boy's Will* the poems tend to take the persona away from people — actually, in dreams or through the imagination. Although Frost found hiding places on the job that inspired the poem, the poem itself deals with the persona among people — albeit only implied people. Hence, the poem simply did not fit the scheme of the book.

The entire poem is filled with visual, auditory and tactile images that hold a good deal of potential, but they are not enough to salvage the sonnet from its own obscurity and a sense that the poem strives too hard for significance. In "Unwilling is the flesh, the spirit weak" and "Upon the soul, still sore from yesterday" I read an attempt to create an illusion of depth where none exists. By merely painting "spirit" and "soul" over what are largely mechanical images Frost has not endowed those images with more depth and heft than they had before — an iron bar painted gold is still an iron bar. Even the reversal of expectations embodied in "Unwilling is the flesh, the spirit weak" is not sufficient to infuse much enthusiasm in the reader. Likewise, the idea of a soul being sore loses, for me, a good deal of the interest it might have produced had it not been so far from its rhyme partner. Closure a bit more epigrammatic might have created a little magic. For all of the activity, the sounds and sensations in the poem, it is remarkably leaden and seems to move more slowly in the sestet despite the increasing number of enjambed lines. The octave plods along as well and seems the very embodiment of its concluding line: "All effort like arising from the dead" — however one reads that line. Even to look at the poem on the page it appears overladen with accented words with too few unaccented syllables to lighten the sound. Yet surprisingly the predominant substitution in the poem is the pyrrhic; there are a scant three spondees. So the sense that the poem is clotted is merely an illusion but an illusion that dominates despite the metrical facts. It is, then, the subject matter itself that creates the illusion of heaviness in direct tension with the whizzing, whirring sound effects in the background — the same background, I might add, where the implied people exist. Even though the poem would not have made it into either of Jarrell's top two classifications, it remains a considerable prosodic achievement insofar as this illusion is concerned.

"The Mill City"

> First published in *Frost: Collected Poems, Prose and Plays*, 1995.

Richard Poirier and Mark Richardson date this poem at 1905. It is an early sonnet, predating the sonnet period of 1906–07 by a year. Like other poems of that time it has a strict Italian octave with a closing couplet.

The octave is a solid piece of writing, even interesting. The out-and-back motion of the poem is a familiar one, and the "blue arc-light" casts a dreamlike, perhaps even hellish, quality over the opening eight lines. The drowned-men image in line six is odd and works no better here than it did in "Despair." How "drowned men" return "from the sea," and walk, even hurry "up from the mills" is problematic at best and unintentionally funny. Were the sestet as strong as the octave, this impossible image might have been the only real weakness in the poem. But the sestet is not strong.

The sestet hinges on supposition and a vague reference to "one hope." There is an echo here of "one wish" in "Into My Own," but here the hope is never spelled out as it is in the other, superior poem. Likewise, the pronoun "one" causes a great deal of confusion here. Are the "ones" of lines nine through eleven the same "One"? "One" in lines nine and ten appear to be the same — referring to "one hope" both times. But the "ones" of line eleven is ambiguous. It might be some animated "hopes" "breasting their current," or it might be the walking drowned men of the octave. It is never made clear.

"Acquainted with the Night" comes to mind because of the similar out-and-back motion of that poem and also the walking that takes place. But there is nothing in "The Mill City" of the qualities that make "Acquainted with the Night" a great poem. Had Frost performed the transforming magic on this poem that he did on "Design," "The Mill City" might have become one of the poems we remember him by. Such is its promise but not its fact.

"Pursuit of the Word"

> According to Poirier and Richardson this is one of seventeen poems Frost sent to Susan Hayes Ward as a Christmas gift in 1911. Published for the first time in *Frost: Collected Poems, Prose and Plays*, 1995.

This poem seems to anticipate a later poem, "Two Tramps in Mud Time," where Frost's notions about singleness and doubleness are given their finest moment anywhere in his canon.

But in "Pursuit of the Word" (note the definite article), exactly what Frost is saying is difficult to ascertain. The single eight-line question of the octave and the single six-line question of the sestet are, as usual in Frost, unanswered and unanswerable. It is not unusual either for Frost to be content with merely asking without hope of an answer, or to create poem-length sentences (see "The Silken Tent") successfully. But here, a combination of long, complicated sentences and unanswerable questions conspire to create a vagueness of response to the poem. Precisely what does he hope to accomplish, to discover, to create by asking these questions? And are the things — objects and abstractions — he places into consideration really valid? "Two ... slippers" and "two birds" and "two vowel sounds" are very different from each other and worlds apart from "pain and mirth" and "Presence and absence." The last two pairs can, in fact, blend into singleness in a life, whereas the slippers, etc. will always remain separate — equal perhaps, but separate. We could stretch the point and say that two slippers make for one well-dressed person, two vowels a well-spoken word, but aren't the two birds always to be separate (unless they mate and produce a new bird)? But is that, finally, the point of the stanza?

If this is Frost "playing," then he has not explained the rules, and the poem is almost annoying in that it insists the reader refer back to the opening line of the octave to understand the direction of the sestet. This is not the typical complexity of a modernist poem, it is simply a feature of a poem more complex and uncertain of itself.

The "yet" that opens the sestet seems to assert that a new twist is about to be added to the opening question, but the question in the sestet is essentially a rewording of the first question. "What, shall there be word single to express" is very simply "Yet none that leaves the vision less than double" restated in such a way as to appear new. But "less than double" can only be single. "Yet," is employed, like many words and phrases in "The Road Not Taken," to suggest something is being stated when in fact it is not. He is not only "fooling himself along" here but fooling us as well. The poem dissolves into a muddle of its own devices.

So, the octave asks if there can be a single "word" and the sestet asserts that vision "weds in utterance what was really one." Yet "Venus and new Moon, water-drop and bubble" are not "one" regardless of what utterance conflates them. They are "one" only insofar as "two eyes make one in sight" — a blessedly simple concept and statement in light of this over-wrought word play.

"The Rain Bath"

> This poem was also part of the Christmas gathering of poems sent to Susan Hayes Ward in 1911. Published for the first time in *Frost: Collected Poems, Prose and Plays*, 1995.

This sonnet is Edenic in setting and its sense of youthful elation at something as simple as rain. Yet, behind all of the naive glee is a powerful storm — "gale," "flood," "tide," "downpour" — and a fear that deliberately or accidentally images the two forces that so powerfully shaped Wordsworth — beauty and fear, as he discusses them in Book One of "The Prelude." There is almost a giddiness, a wildness that is barely contained here. Truly, opposites are held in mind at the same time and the mood of the poem swings back and forth between them.

If it were not for some vagueness in places — who is being addressed? why are they in a house "in camp"?— this too might have been a famous Frost poem. It is energetic, relatively free of obscurities and contains a nearly memorable closing couplet. Yet, at best, this poem belongs only among those that deserve a reading. The archaic "sylvan roof," the horse imagery of line three, and the vague "frolic fear" of line six combine to dampen the overall effect of the poem. It feels forced, not the organic melting down from delight to wisdom that we perceive in the best sonnets. Most of the poem sounds fresh and natural. Even the light mood against the fearsome backdrop of the setting feels right. But there is also a consciously shaping mind at work here tinkering with the unconscious flow of words. "Frolic fear" is self-conscious, too obviously contrived to alliterate with "flood" in the first hemistich.

Finally, the poem leaves the impression that it was "worried into being" as Frost says a poem cannot be. Perhaps it is the poet's own fault, but he has led us to expect to delight in original, unaffected line and image, and when he manipulates those (and the reader) we are unforgiving. There is a sense of play, a sense of talk — high marks! high marks!— but the phoniness of a few fill-in-the-blank phrases spoils the performance.

"On Talk of Peace at This Time"

> "This poem was inscribed in a copy of *Mountain Interval* (1916) given to Mark Anthony DeWolfe Howe in December 1916"(Poirier and Richardson 992). Appeared in *Robert Frost 100*, 1974, compiled by Edward Connery Lathem. Reprinted in *Frost: Collected Poems, Prose and Plays*, 1995.

This sonnet, written in 1916, more resembles the sonnets in the "Editorials" section of *Steeple Bush* (194) than it does the remarkable sonnets of *Mountain Interval*. It is an early predictor of the really weak political poetry Frost would write after World War II.

At a time when some truly magnificent modernist poetry was

coming from Owen, Brooke, Sassoon, Graves and others, this poem is more of the ilk from nonparticipants writing from a safe distance and cheering on the soldiers through their bloodbaths. It is patriotic to the extent that alliances create fellow feelings in tough situations.

In a large sense this is a very selfish poem, one that encourages France to continue to supply cannon fodder to make things comfy for those already safely tucked away in unaffected places in the world. "France. France. I know not what is in my heart," rings as false as anything in his canon, and by the end of the poem what is in his heart is quite well known. He gives France a grand-gesture slap on the back — "But I will not believe that you will cease" — and then, with eyes averted, slips in his willingness to let France make the world a safer place.

I would not want to be a Frenchman reading this poem. There is no inner or outer humor, just inner and outer seriousness. Unless Frost is writing this with his tongue planted very deeply in his cheek, the sentiment is almost too cold to contemplate. Perhaps militarily it was wise to continue the fighting until it was done, but to encourage more death for a country that was already nearly destroyed seems morally abhorrent. There was that side of Frost — evident in "No Holy Wars for Them" — but there is no other evidence for such a blighted attitude at this date. And there is nothing here to make us believe this was tongue-in-cheek; it is heart-felt but sentimental and misguided.

The sonnet is strict English with an unmemorable couplet. Only the odd, weak use of "distorted" bears mentioning. This is one of those rare instances in Frost where rhyme manipulates a word choice that is barely acceptable. "Distorted" weakens France's effort, as if it were fighting for some mere principle or ideology rather than the very real "mortal stakes." The image/statement is vague, made so by "everything" — a typical Frost hedge — "that might have been distorted." The conditional "might" further weakens the line, allowing it only to hint at anything really solidly or possibly threatening. Of course the threat was very real, as was the attack, but the poem skirts that, opting instead for a watered-down suggestion. This line, unfortunately, functions much like the entire poem. Upon a cursory reading it appears that something is actually being said, but upon closer scrutiny that statement is elusive, vague and most likely worthy of contempt no matter how deeply and genuinely it may have been felt.

"The Pans"

> Written ca. 1926 and first published in *Frost: Collected Poems, Prose and Plays*, 1995.

Except for the alexandrine first line, this is a strict English sonnet with the odd but emphatic turn at line nine. Line ten draws a great deal of attention to the turn with a noisiness found only rarely in Frost's poems. The "And clang! clang-clang! clang-clang! down through the night" is as raucous, and I think overtly humorous, as we ever find him being. He is saying, here in a poem, what he argued vigorously and seriously in letters and conversations: we need justice over mercy, that mercy is weakness, but we are, perhaps, only entitled to mercy after the fall.

In a letter to Wilbert Snow in January 1938, Frost commented on these lines from Milton: "... in Mercy and Justice both, / Through Heav'n and Earth, so shall my glorie excel, / But Mercy first and last shall brightest shine." Said Frost: "You know your Milton and your Puritanism. He used it in the sense of first aid to what? To the deserving? No, to the totally depraved and undeserving. That's what we are and have been since the day Eve ate the rotten apple. ...'In Adam's fall We sinned all.' Mercy ensued.... Illogical kindness — that is Mercy" (quoted in Thompson *Later Years* 403–4).

The humor, of course, is of the darkest sort. The poem asserts that even one who desires justice (the "I" of the poem) somehow shrinks from it, perhaps out of generational habit. The relaxation and resignation of the first quatrain give way to a cringing in the second and a flinching in the third, an odd progression that presumably grows out of the blindness he is stricken with in line two. The request by "the voice" for him to "Hold out your hand ... for the surprise" and the later "A penny for your thoughts" mimic an adult speaking to a small child. Likewise the cringing and flinching are a child's reaction to fearful situations. This kind of treatment by "the voice" suggests that that is all we've come to deserve, since we have come to expect mercy. In this sense the childness of man is in keeping with his belief in utter subordination. As Thompson points out in regard to Frost's hope that his offering of poetry at the altar would be good enough in the eyes of God: "that hope, as placed by him in that context, reflects his essentially self-abasing belief that wormlike man is so evil, at all times, that he cannot escape the deserved and eternal punishment of God, except by means of that eternal salvation which is provided only through the mercy and grace of God" (Thompson *Years of Triumph* 568).

With that in mind the "was to have been..." and "Was to have had..." of lines twelve and thirteen are both wistful sounding, too-mild laments for the potentially powerful justice that has been lost. The persona (strongly Frostian in belief) mirrors statements expressed in letters and conversations that justice is not possible, only mercy is available to us — "Illogical kindness." There is a dark resignation to the fact. A sorrow and an irony. Like Gawain he flinches at the blow. But there is no second chance. Flinch, and you lose. That is justice. The irony is in the fact that he regrets the justice of not getting a second chance. This strongly suggests that we have come around to expecting mercy even when we say we want justice.

"It was a trust," he says in lines eleven and fourteen, but that too is wistful, for the "trust" was only ever given to Adam and Eve, who lost it for all of us. So the wistful mourning of "trust" in the past tense also suggests a learned or inherited desire for something he never had.

That Frost took this conflict between justice and mercy as seriously as anything in his life is borne out by a line from the last letter he wrote, less than two days before he died.

"How can we be just," he wrote to G. R. Elliott on January 27, 1963, "in a world that needs mercy and merciful in a world that needs justice?" (quoted in Thompson, *Later Years* 344).

The choice of the sonnet form for this poem is an interesting one. In no way can the sonnet be thought of as a merciful form. Its demands are many, as Frost discussed at some length in "The Constant Symbol." Can the sonnet then be said to be a just form? Well, to the extent that any fixed form can be equated to law, and in that its demands are such that the laws of the sonnet give direction and remove certain decisions from the creative process, then the sonnet is just. Any poet may choose another form — a ballad or free verse, say — and ignore the sonnet's laws, but if the sonnet is the form chosen then it is, in a large sense, just. Were it unjust, poets would have more than likely abandoned it long ago as they have largely abandoned other forms, such as the triolet and the rondeau. The poem then says,

"If I cannot have 'the gift of being just,' if I cannot be 'justice on a height,' then I can at least do justice to the sonnet form." And justice might have been done to this sonnet had a few of the poem's problems been addressed during revision. But they were not. The poem was lost, abandoned or forgotten, and it remains full of unrealized potential. Despite that, it is among the best of the uncollected sonnets and may some day have an audience.

"Trouble Rhyming"

> Written ca. 1930; first appeared in *The Letters of Robert Frost to Louis Untermeyer*, 1963. Reprinted in *Frost: Complete Poems, Prose and Plays*, 1995.

This is "play" at its purest. The sonnet was written around a prearranged list of fourteen words provided by light verse poet Burges Johnson (Poirier and Richardson 993). According to Louis Untermeyer, "Although Robert willingly complied, he burlesqued the whole idea" (quoted in Poirier and Richardson 993).

Frost's love of games is certainly in evidence here, and the reader is invited to participate in making some literal sense of the poem by substituting puns, homonyms, mis- and foreign pronunciations, slang and technical meanings for the rhyme words provided. In lines one and two we must read "hole" for "whole" and "suite" for "sweet." In line three the "Scotch friend" may say "Greet, oh Greet," but we are to hear "great."

In line four Frost transposes the "o" and "a" in "goal" to create "gaol" the British variant of "jail." "Roll" is used in its slang sense in line five, as is "neat" in line seven. The sixth line's "feet" is used technically—metrical feet. Read "sole" for "soul," and hear "slip" for "sleep" ("as the French say in English") in lines eight and nine. Then hear "fox pass" for "faux pas" ("as we might say in French"). "No" is "know," "Deep" is "deep." Read "a lass" for "alas" and see "go" merely separated from its fellow syllables. As sonnets go it is obscure and nonliteral but great fun to untangle with a dictionary and a healthy application of imagination. It is a strict Italian sonnet with no exceptional metrical substitutions — but who's paying attention when there is other fun to be had?

Where many of the uncollected sonnets fail from trying too hard, or not hard enough, "Trouble Rhyming" succeeds because it doesn't pretend to anything more than game, play, fun and a pure reveling in the nuances and peculiarities of our language — and those who use it.

"A Bed in the Barn"

> Written ca. 1944–1947; first appeared in *Robert Frost: A Descriptive Catalogue of Books and Manuscripts* in the Clifton Waller Barrett Library, University of Virginia, 1974, edited by Joan St. C. Crane (Poirier and Richardson 962). Originally part of *Steeple Bush*, 1947, but removed before publication. Reprinted in *Frost: Collected Poems, Prose and Plays*, 1995.

Because of the tetrameter lines and the very regular iambic meter — with anapests the most common substitutions in lines one through five, eight through ten and perhaps twelve — there is a singsong quality to the poem that Frost usually avoided or reserved for special occasions such as mockery. It seems curious that this poem was removed from *Steeple Bush* because it is much better than many of the sonnets that were collected there. At first glance it also appears as if the poem would have fit nicely into the "Editorials" section with the other social commentary.

But so much for appearances and "seems." What at first looks like another occasion for anecdote and an insightful comment is really the occasion for more than that. In the mid-forties, following the death of Elinor, Frost was very much a tramp himself, staying with friends and acquaintances when he visited colleges, even going so far as to invite himself at times. According to Thompson he was a gracious guest, repaying hospitality with gifts and small kindnesses. In this sense he is "tramp polite."

But this poem is also a kind of self-effacing gesture, a nod to the public man he had become. And before he lost sight of that he retained the ability to take a poke at himself as a reminder not to take himself too seriously. The movement of the poem seems to support the idea that this is precisely what he is doing here. The octave is a third-person anecdote about a tramp seeking a bed for the night, willingly surrendering pipe and matches as gesture of his honesty and safety. The sestet is a first-person meditation on the tramp's gesture and on self-evaluation. The concluding couplet, however, shifts to second person and looks very much like self-address. "For you're sadly apt to overdo / Your praise when wholly left to you." The vernacular shift to "you" can be seen as a sign of self-consciousness, and Frost's self-promotion during this period occasionally made him aware of how far he had come from the near-hermit lifestyle of the Derry years.

The couplets of "A Bed in the Barn" connect it to "Into My Own" and "Once by the Pacific," though the prophetic nature of these two poems is not picked up. The tetrameter lines, and the anecdote-then-commentary format of the poem bring it closer to "Unharvested." Either way, it has echoes of earlier sonnets. If this poem finds an audience, is perhaps anthologized, the epigrammatic closure is likely to become a catch phrase, lines as memorable as those that conclude "Design," "Once by the Pacific" or "Into My Own."

Because none of the other "Editorials" turn inward to such a degree as "A Bed in the Barn," it seems more obvious, on closer scrutiny, why this poem was removed from *Steeple Bush*, despite its being superior. Frost would have had no qualms about sacrificing it for the continuity of the book.

It should surprise no one that Frost withheld these poems from publication. They are certainly not a *serious* embarrassment to their author, but they also, in general, add little to the larger canon or to the sonnets as a group. Although it is possible that a few of these sonnets, "A Bed in the Barn" and "The Pans," will find an audience, it is not likely that they will unseat any of the poems currently anthologized on a regular basis.

So this chapter has been an experiment, an experiment that carried with it a modicum of hope of discovering a misjudged or mishandled masterpiece. It did not. Yet neither did the experiment fail. In the process of examination, I have given these poems more attention than they have received in the past. This survey, cursory as it is, should put to rest any little nagging doubts — if there should even be any — that we have perhaps missed something.

By including these sonnets with the twenty-eight Robert Frost did publish, and by making available this brief commentary, we have perhaps allowed the truly great sonnets in the canon to shine that much brighter. Our appreciation for the craft, the seemingly carefree play and the way delight becomes wisdom can only deepen when the merely third- or fourth-best is juxtaposed to the fine and extraordinary.

Bibliography

Barry, Elaine. *Robert Frost*. New York: Frederick Ungar, 1973.
Cook, Reginald L. "Robert Frost." *Sixteen Modern American Authors*. Ed. Jackson R. Meyer. New York: Norton, 1973. 323–365
Doyle, John Robert, Jr. *The Poetry of Robert Frost*. New York: Hafner, 1962.
Frost, Robert. *Complete Poems of Robert Frost*. New York: Holt, Rinehart and Winston, 1968.
——. *Frost: Collected Poems, Prose and Plays*. Ed. Richard Poirier and Mark Richardson. New York: Library of America, 1995.
Fussell, Paul. *Poetic Meter and Poetic Form*. New York: Random House, 1968.
Holland, Norman N. *The Brain of Robert Frost*. New York: Routledge, 1988.
Isaacs, Elizabeth. *An Introduction to Robert Frost*. Denver: Alan Swallow, 1962.
Jarrell, Randall. *Poetry and the Age*. New York: Alfred A. Knopf, 1953.
Lentricchia, Frank. *Robert Frost: Modern Poetics and the Landscape of Self*. Durham, NC: Duke University Press, 1975.
Montiero, George. "Robert Frost's Metaphysical Sonnet." *Centennial Essays*. Ed. Jac Tharpe. Jackson: University Press of Mississippi, 1974. 333–339
Nitchie, George W. *Human Values in the Poetry of Robert Frost*. Durham, NC: Duke University Press, 1960.
Poirier, Richard. *Robert Frost: The Work of Knowing*. New York: Oxford University Press, 1977.
Pritchard, William H. *Frost: A Literary Life Reconsidered*. Amherst, MA: University of Massachusetts Press, 1984.
Stout, Janis P. "Convention and Variation in Frost's Sonnets." *Concerning Poetry*, Vol. 2, no. 1 (Spring 1978).
Thompson, Lawrance. *Robert Frost: The Early Years*. New York: Holt, Rinehart and Winston, 1966.
——. *Robert Frost: The Years of Triumph*. New York: Holt, Rinehart and Winston, 1970.
Thompson, Lawrance, and R. H. Winnick. *Robert Frost: The Later Years*. New York: Holt, Rinehart and Winston, 1976.
Thoreau, Henry David. *Walden*. New York: Holt, Rinehart and Winston, 1965.
Warren, Robert Penn. *Selected Essays*. New York: Random House, 1958.
Westbrook, Perry. "Robert Frost's New England." *Centennial Essays*. Ed. Jac Tharpe. Jackson: University Press of Mississippi, 1974. 239–255

Index

"Acceptance" 61–64, 69, 71, 73, 83, 95, 96, 97, 109
"Acquainted with the Night" 7, 12, 17, 30, 69, 70, 71, 73, 83, 95, 97, 117, 142
"After Apple Picking" 119
"Any Size We Please" 118–120

Barry, Elaine 4, 7, 8, 11, 76, 92, 93
"A Bed in the Barn" 141–142
"Bereft" 73, 76, 97, 123
Bogan, Louise 75
A Boy's Will 3, 11, 12, 25, 28, 29, 30, 32, 34, 37, 42, 55, 129, 132
"The Broken Drought" 123–125
"Bursting Rapture" 122–123, 130

Complete Poems 3, 7, 11, 28
"A Considerable Speck" 50
"The Constant Symbol" 5, 6, 130, 139
couplets 3, 96, 106, 118, 119, 142
Crane, Stephen 63, 74

"Desert Places" 76
"Design" 12, 19, 32, 67, 68, 71, 72, 73, 89–94, 95, 96, 97, 103, 106, 108, 111, 117, 130, 134, 142
"Despair" 129–131
DeVoto, Bernard 25
"Directive" 115, 124
Doyle, John R., Jr. 68, 72–75, 79, 80

"A Dream Pang" 17, 28–31, 130
Eliot, T.S. 16, 23, 94, 124
"Etherealizing" 115–116, 118, 120

"The Figure a Poem Makes" 4, 5, 70, 110, 111
"The Flood" 69–72, 77, 82, 89, 95
Frost: Collected Poems, Prose and Plays 11, 12
A Further Range 8, 11, 87–99
Fussell, Paul 7, 31

"The Gift Outright" 7

"Home Burial" 116
"Hyla Brook" 6, 37, 74

In the Clearing 11, 25, 55
"In White" 32, 90, 93, 94, 130
"Into My Own" 3, 12, 17, 23–28, 30, 33, 41, 42, 73, 95, 124, 133, 142
"The Investment" 79–83, 121
Isaacs, Elizabeth 75, 76, 92

Jarrell, Randall 3, 9, 15, 17, 76, 78, 82, 89, 90, 93, 115, 124

King Jasper 15, 49

Lentricchia, Frank 73, 74, 91
"A Line Gang" 37

A Masque of Mercy 118–120
A Masque of Reason 118–120
"The Master Speed" 9, 87–89, 99
"Meeting and Passing" 337–40, 45, 63, 111
"The Mill City" 133–134
Montiero, George 89, 93, 94
"The Most of It" 32, 76, 96, 106, 119, 129
"The Mountain" 32, 80
Mountain Interval 11, 37–50, 136
"Mowing" 7, 8, 16, 37, 43

"Neither Out Far Nor In Deep" 48, 78, 97
"Never Again Would Birds' Song Be the Same" 12, 31, 106–109
New Hampshire 11, 53–57
Nitchie, George 74, 75
"No Holy Wars for Them" 121–122, 137
North of Boston 11, 30, 46

"On a Bird Singing in Its Sleep" 18, 26, 31, 94–98, 109
"On a Tree Fallen Across the Road" 19, 53–57, 63, 64, 69, 80
"On Talk of Peace at This Time" 136–137
"Once by the Pacific" 12, 18, 26, 65–69, 70, 71, 73, 83, 95, 97, 117, 142
"The Oven Bird" 9, 10, 12, 17, 30, 31, 40–44, 95, 96, 97, 108, 109, 111

"The Pans" 138–140
"The Pasture" 23, 46
Petrarch, Francesco 7, 103
"The Planners" 120–121
Richard Poirier 75, 89, 90, 91, 97, 133, 134, 136, 140, 141
Pound, Ezra 16
Pritchard, William 7, 48, 67, 70, 76, 79, 103, 109, 117, 119, 121, 129, 131
"Pursuit of the Word" 134–135
"Putting in the Seed" 12, 44–48

"The Rain Bath" 135–136
"Range-Finding" 48–50, 64, 111
Renga 10, 11
"The Road Not Taken" 25, 32, 62, 95, 135
Robinson, Edwin Arlington 15, 24

"The Secret Sits" 18
"A Servant to Servants" 74
Shakespeare, William 6, 7, 31, 44, 87, 103, 108, 110, 122
"The Silken Tent" 12, 68, 70, 77, 103–106, 109, 117, 120, 134
"A Soldier" 77–79, 82, 89, 111
Steeple Bush 8, 11, 12, 95, 111, 115–125, 136, 141
Stevens, Wallace 16
"Stopping by Woods on a Snowy Evening" 88
Stout, Janis P. 3, 4, 7, 8
Strong Measures 10
"The Subverted Flower" 45

terza rima 3, 7, 10, 72–77
Thompson, Lawrance 24, 28, 30, 37, 39, 53, 66, 70, 74, 76, 79, 94, 103, 118, 122, 124, 129, 131, 132, 138, 139, 141
Thoreau, Henry David 47
"Time Out" 109-111
"To the Right Person" 8
"The Trial by Existence" 61, 63, 67, 79, 123
"Trouble Rhyming" 140–141
"Turn" 5, 7, 8, 28, 31, 33, 39, 43, 50, 63, 82, 87, 103, 106, 121, 138
"Two Look at Two" 119

"Unharvested" 8, 9, 10, 88, 98–99, 109, 110, 116, 142
Untermeyer, Louis 6, 24, 62, 69, 88, 89, 140

"The Vantage Point" 7, 8, 17, 18, 19, 31–34, 48, 68
Voices and Visions 7, 73, 106

Ward, Susan Hayes 28, 48, 89, 129, 134, 135
Warren, Robert Penn 27

Westbrook, Perry 61
West-Running Brook 11, 61–83, 87, 88, 95
"When the Speed Comes" 131–133
"Why Wait for Science" 116–118, 120, 124
Williams, William Carlos 16
A Witness Tree 11, 103–111
Wordsworth, William 23, 31, 65, 66, 135
Wylie, Elinor 9

Yeats, William Butler 23, 67

www.ingramcontent.com/pod-product-compliance
Ingram Content Group UK Ltd.
Pitfield, Milton Keynes, MK11 3LW, UK
UKHW042017140426
5217IPUK00015B/1218

9 780786 424207